People are talking

"Sister Valerie Schneider has developed a most helpful book for catechists who teach sacraments to high school students. I found the approach of presenting the teaching, followed by prayers, and concluding with suggested activities, to be very helpful. This book contains solid sacramental theology with a focus on historical development. The reader will find a sense of freshness in the proposed activities."

†James R. Hoffman
Bishop of Toledo

"*Teaching Sacraments and Seasons* is a valuable resource for religion teachers and catechists. In a concise, user friendly way, Sr. Valerie Schneider takes familiar material about the sacraments and liturgical seasons and presents it in new, creative ways. I especially like the format in which she does this: each chapter begins with a story which provides a theological or historical perspective; next come simple, yet creative prayers flowing from the chapter theme; finally, concluding activities give students ample opportunities to connect the contents of the chapter with their lived experience.

"It is my hope that *Teaching Sacraments and Seasons* will help students and teachers alike come to a deeper realization that all of life is sacramental, holy, and redeemed."

Sr. Miriam Eble, SND
Assistant Superintendent of Religious Education
Diocese of Toledo, Ohio

"Sr. Valerie Schneider's book is a boon to teachers who are looking for new activities to add sparkle to old lesson plans. Of special interest and helpfulness are the introductory sections to each topic. These supply historical and theological information in a pleasing, informal manner that makes the material easy to digest. Teachers will also appreciate the prepared prayers and prayer services related to the chapter themes."

Mary Kathleen Glavich, SND
Author of *Weekday Liturgies for Children*
and *Prayer Moments for Every Day of the Year*

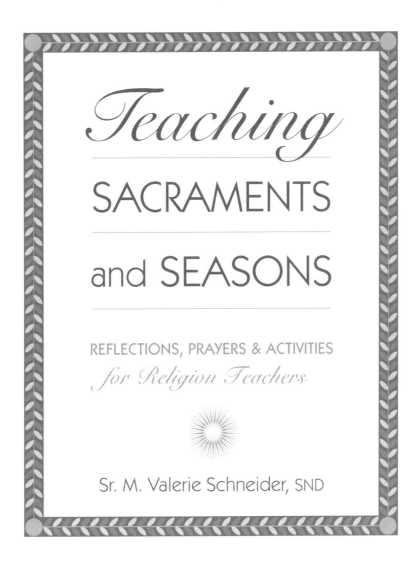

Teaching

SACRAMENTS

and SEASONS

REFLECTIONS, PRAYERS & ACTIVITIES
for Religion Teachers

Sr. M. Valerie Schneider, SND

XXIII

TWENTY-THIRD PUBLICATIONS
Mystic, CT 06355

Dedication

To the faculty and students of
St. John High School, Delphos, Ohio.

Twenty-Third Publications
185 Willow Street
P.O. Box 180
Mystic, CT 06355
(860) 536-2611
(800) 321-0411

ISBN: 0-89622-985-8
Library of Congress Catalog Card Number: 99-71171
Printed in the U.S.A.

Table of Contents

Teaching Sacraments and Seasons

Introduction

I have been a teacher at the middle school and high school level for most of my teaching career. As such, I have probably taught 5000 religion classes, from grades six through twelve, during this time. But even with this background, I was not quite prepared for what I would find one day when I was asked to be a substitute teacher for grade two at a summer Bible school.

These seven and eight year olds were in my care for three hours: pretty scary stuff for a high school teacher! I did know one thing that would need to be a part of my lesson plan for that day, which was that I should keep changing the learning activity. Yet when my young charges fidgeted the first time, I almost panicked.

Miraculously, the idea of a "God-parade" came to me. I had the children line up, then we walked around the room praising and thanking God, calling out "Hooray for God! Three cheers for God!" When we finished, the second graders practically screamed with pleasure: "We never did that before!" Even though their religious education had spanned only two years, they appreciated the newness.

This incident made me realize again how hard we teachers have to work to keep religious instruction new. While praising and thanking God was probably an "old" concept for these second-graders, the parade was new. And therein lies the purpose of this book: to provide the parade. In this case, it is to take familiar material about the sacraments and liturgical seasons and cast it in a new light, present it in new ways.

I have taken those areas of sacraments and the seasons that are most frequently taught and have tried to give teacher background and classroom activities that might provide new approaches to "old" topics. Depending upon one's educational background, the material may either be new, or else provide a new vocabulary.

Each chapter begins with a brief catechetical essay on a particular topic, drawing out the main points from an historical and theological perspective. The essay is followed by prayer experiences and suggested activities, each of which will help students better understand the truths of their faith, then incorporate them into their daily lives. There is also a page at the end of the chapter for your own notes and ideas.

You won't find every sacrament or liturgical topic in this book, of course. Time and space do not allow such expansiveness here. Essays on the sacraments include those most often taught in the intermediate and junior high grades: namely, baptism, confirmation, eucharist, and reconciliation. Because holy orders, matrimony, and the anointing of the sick are not so frequently presented, they are in less need of new and creative ideas. Sometimes they become part of a special course in high school, such as Lifestyles or Death and Dying; surely, their omission from this book is not a reflection on their importance.

Similarly, essays on the church year (also called the liturgical year) do not include ordinary time, because the topic is not so frequently addressed in a school setting. The seasons of Advent, Christmas, Lent, and Easter, on the other hand, are presented every year. "How can I talk about Lent in a new way this year?" may well be a question teachers ask as they prepare their lesson plans. This book will help construct an answer to that question.

In learning about sacraments, students will begin to see them as a sign of redemption happening in our midst, a ritualization of the Paschal Mystery, the whole life of Christ. Further, sacraments help establish a relationship with the church. As Edward Kilmartin writes in *The Sacraments: God's Love and Mercy Actualized*, sacraments are "essential engagements with Jesus Christ in the Spirit with the community of believers." Students growing in their faith need to grow in their realization that the community *is* Christ, for it is "the incarnational prolongation of the mission of the saving Christ" (Jerome Murphy-O'Connor, *Eucharist and Community in First Corinthians*).

This book intends to place the sacraments and liturgical seasons in the context of a big picture; that is, how to live fully human lives, the kind of lives modeled by Christ throughout his time here on earth. What Christ did in and for the world of his day, Christianity—specifically for most of us, the Catholic Church—does in and for our world today. The underlying assumption of this book is the basic tenet of St. Paul's theology: the true nature of the Christian community is its identity with Christ. We are Christians because we belong to the body of Christ. It is through the church, this particular community of Christians, that we meet Christ, salvation is mediated, and the word is given.

To find Christ in our world, we need only look around. Let us start now with the sacraments and seasons.

CHAPTER ONE

Sacraments

Ritual Moments in Living the Life of Christ

One year, a terrible winter storm hit our area right after New Year's Day. This gave our schools ten more free—and completely unexpected—days at the end of Christmas vacation. Exams were postponed, pushing the second semester almost into February. Superintendents and principals worried about making up the lost days. Coaches worried about the readiness of their athletes after many missed practices. Teachers were concerned about being on time for annual spring projects. All of us, students and faculty alike, needed something to get the school back on track.

Somehow, I was inspired to conduct a non-sacramental healing service on the first day of the new semester. Many in the school were eager for this opportunity to gather together in prayer. Star players injured in football season were still not in shape for winter sports. Other students struggled in their studies and dreaded another long semester. One teacher had cancer. A number of friends and relatives of staff and students were experiencing unusual medical problems. The time was right to focus on mental, physical, and spiritual healing.

The religion department invited two women from the local parish to speak to the students. Each one approached the topic of healing from a different perspective. The first woman, who was the bus driver for many of the students, spoke of her parents and the pain she endured because they had never said "I love you" to her. The second woman, whose sons had recently graduated from our school, talked about the alcoholism of one of her sons. Throughout these stories, the students sat spellbound, many with tears in their eyes. All identified in some way with the stories.

When the women had finished speaking, each grade level, freshmen through senior, formed a separate group on the gym floor. The teachers formed a fifth group. Ten or so people from outside the school and who were known for their charismatic gifts were also present at the healing service. Two of them went into each of the five groups, and prayed over anyone who asked.

What we thought would take ten minutes lasted for an hour. The entire gym was electrified with the presence of God. The seniors were the first to disband, but they quickly joined the outer circles of the other three classes as a sign of their solidarity. When all circles were back in their seats and the final prayer had been said, the principal came forward to dismiss the students. He was, however, speechless. We learned that day that almost anything can precipitate a sacramental moment—not just the seven sacraments.

The sacramental life of the church

It was the Second Vatican Council which made us aware that all is sacramental, when the Council emphasized liturgical theology over sacramental theology. The difference between the two approaches is tremendous. Sacramental theology emphasizes the power of words in objective rites, causality, the proof of how grace causes certain effects, the manner in which Christ in heaven is also the Christ in the communion wafers, and so on. But when the Holy Spirit blew open the windows during Vatican II, so to speak, and brought in the fresh *ruah* (spirit), we began to address our faith in terms of liturgical theology.

Today we emphasize how the sacraments express the mystery of Christ and the real nature of the true church. Before Vatican II, sacraments were considered "things"; now they are considered lively expressions by which the whole church embodies and makes accessible the saving work of Christ. Liturgical theology explores the interface between sacramental rituals and the human life. And because God became incarnate and made the church an extension of himself, the whole life of the church is sacramental—not just its seven chief rites.

As teachers we need to be careful that we never reduce liturgical theology to the sacraments. Such minimalism does not allow our students to express and celebrate all that makes up the life of faith. There is danger that first eucharist, first reconciliation, or confirmation become events which the church celebrates occasionally when certain groups are ready, instead of being the premier way in which the Triune God communicates. Students need to know that they habitually live in God, but they encounter God most specifically in the sacraments.

Sacraments are close encounters with God, engaging us with Christ. For Christ is the full expression of the profoundest engagement of God with the world. What God intended in creation is done in Christ. Jesus is the norm for all encounters with God. This makes Christ the primordial sacrament. As Michael Schmaus writes in *The Church as Sacrament*: "Jesus Christ is the ultimate sign of God's salvation in the world [for the] man Jesus Christ is the locus and the means of God's encounter with man. Thus we call him the original sacrament.... In him there is the total self-communication of God and the total human response to it."

A human encounter with God

Please note that the locus of sacraments lies in the human nature of Jesus, and not in the Logos. The incarnation is the basis of all sacraments; if God had not become human, sacraments would be an absurdity. Edward Schillebeeckx states in *Christ the Sacrament of the Encounter with God*: "Human encounter with Jesus is therefore the sacrament of the encounter with God." Jesus is the only way to redemption.

While Jesus is the primordial sacrament, the church (God's people) is the fundamental sacrament. The primary place where we meet God is in the assembly of the baptized. This is just another way of stating that Christ is the head, we the members; Christ is the vine, we the branches. There is a close association between the work of the church as it assembles for worship and the work of Christ redeeming us. When the assembly worships, Christ stands as the chief liturgist. When the church baptizes, Christ baptizes. When the priest gives absolution, God forgives sin. When the bishop anoints, God sets his seal.

As stated before, all of the church's life is sacrament, not just the seven chief rites. When the church actualizes her essence as the fundamental sacrament of grace, there we have sacrament. When the presence of God is most seen in the people, rather than in the rites, we can say with Edward Kilmartin: "The essential Christian engagement is: Christ for us! We with Christ!"

Christ was with us during the healing service in the gym on the first day of the new semester, without doubt. For weeks after this service, parents called to say that their son or daughter couldn't stop talking about the event. This is evidence of the power of a sacramental moment. The faculty and staff planning this event never imagined the impact the service would have on the students. It showed us—and them—that the power of God is present with us, always.

Prayer

Litany Honoring the Role of Jesus Christ in the Sacraments

Divide the students into two groups. Have one group say the common response, and another group read the roles of Jesus. Or designate several readers for the various roles, with the other students repeating, "We praise you, Jesus…."

Group 1	Group 2
We praise you, Jesus…	the sign of God's salvation in the world.
We praise you, Jesus…	perfect unity of word and sacrament.
We praise you, Jesus…	the "place" where the church is called together.
We praise you, Jesus…	total self-communication of God.
We praise you, Jesus…	total human response to God.
We praise you, Jesus…	the primary sacrament.
We praise you, Jesus…	the one through whom we have our being.
We praise you, Jesus…	the norm of all encounters with God.
We praise you, Jesus…	the perfection of creation.
We praise you, Jesus…	the full expression of God's involvement with us.
We praise you, Jesus…	for the mysteries of your life.
We praise you, Jesus…	for sharing your priesthood with us.
We praise you, Jesus…	for sending your disciples to baptize.
We praise you, Jesus…	for forming a people through your word.
We praise you, Jesus…	through whose power the sacraments are effective.
We praise you, Jesus…	sign of the covenant.
We praise you, Jesus…	healer of sickness and sin.
We praise you, Jesus…	for divine forgiveness.

Group 1	Group 2
We praise you, Jesus…	the one who baptizes through the church.
We praise you, Jesus…	for your baptism in the Jordan River.
We praise you, Jesus…	for bringing us to birth in baptism.
We praise you, Jesus…	for the gifts of your Holy Spirit.
We praise you, Jesus…	for giving us yourself as food.
We praise you, Jesus…	bread for the life of the world.
We praise you, Jesus…	whose whole life was an offering.
We praise you, Jesus…	whose sacrifice gave us the eucharist.
We praise you, Jesus…	truly present in the consecrated bread and wine.
We praise you, Jesus…	for offering the eucharistic sacrifice.
We praise you, Jesus…	for your presence in the ministerial priesthood.
We praise you, Jesus…	for blessing the marriage covenant.
We praise you, Jesus…	for being the head of the church.
We praise you, Jesus…	for being the model of what we should become.
We praise you, Jesus…	for your presence in all who worship you.
We praise you, Jesus…	for your life of grace.
We praise you, Jesus…	for yourself. Amen.

Activities

1. Where do you live?

Go around the classroom and ask several students where they live. Most students will respond with the name of a town, or say "right here," "in a house," "on Earth," and so on. After each response, say, "I'm sorry. You forgot." Then remind them that they live in God.

Tell the students that because we live in God our whole life is sacramental, whether we play sports, clean our room, do homework, or shop. We should become aware that everything we do is an opportunity to meet God. Discuss with the class different ways that the students encounter God during the ordinary—and extraordinary—events and occurrences of daily life.

2. Sacraments are a process

Sacraments are more than special blessings received in a church building and usually forgotten once outside. Sacraments are a process, for every sacrament has a before, during, and after.

One way to emphasize this continuing action is to use "-ing" verbs. Briefly review the differences among present tense, past tense, present perfect tense, and progressive verb forms. So often we speak of sacraments in the past tense: "I was baptized when I was a month old." Sometimes it is the present perfect tense: "Yes, I have been confirmed." Sometimes it is the present tense: "I am a baptized Christian." But the progressive verb forms bring the power of the sacrament home to us in a very immediate way: we are always being baptized, we are always being married, we are always being reconciled, ordained, and healed. The -ing form shows that the effects of the sacraments are always with us; we can constantly live in the grace of the sacraments we have received.

3. We live the whole life of Christ

When Jesus told his disciples, "Do this in memory of me," he was not referring solely to the consecration of bread and wine. This statement invites us to live the whole life of Christ, his attitudes and actions, his time here on earth, his dying, rising, exaltation, and sending of the Spirit. The mystery of Christ celebrated in a sacrament must be the mystery we live.

Discuss with students the attitudes and behaviors they must assume upon the reception of each of the seven sacraments. For example, in baptism we take on the role of priest, prophet, and royalty in God's kingdom. In matrimony, we become witnesses to God's love for his people. Then discuss how we can adopt and adapt these attitudes and behaviors throughout our lives, whether at work, play, or study.

4. Put learning to work

Instead of taking a test after the study of each sacrament, put a more practical spin on your evaluation. Here are a few examples:

• After studying matrimony, have the students write a commentary on the sacrament that can be read before the nuptial Mass or inserted in the wedding program, or prepare a brief homily on marriage.

• Let the students interview persons who have received the sacrament of anointing. Ask them to base their questions on what you have studied about this sacrament. The students can then compare the responses of the persons interviewed with their own views of the sacrament.

•Students can make a timeline of the historical development of the sacrament of reconciliation. Have them continue the timeline into the next millennium and predict what the sacrament might look like in the future.

• Help the students dramatize highlights of an ordination ceremony. (Call your diocesan liturgy office for guidelines.) You or your students may want to capture the dramatization on videotape.

Notes

CHAPTER TWO

Baptism

An Historical Overview

Right before the start of the Easter Vigil one year in our parish, a small fire broke out in an electrical box in the basement of the church. The fire caused the loss of over ninety percent of the power in the church building, leaving only one line operating—the electricity for the organ.

Because the Vigil begins in darkness, most of the assembly was not aware of the loss of electrical power. The presider, lectors, and choir members kept their candles, lit from the paschal fire, going throughout the long Liturgy of the Word. The readings and homily were proclaimed and preached without a microphone; the psalmist used lung power she never knew she had. Meanwhile, two electricians who had been miraculously scheduled as greeters for the Vigil worked in the basement.

As the power had not yet been restored, the Rites of Initiation began in darkness. The Litany of Saints was sung, the water was blessed, and the elect professed their faith. Next came the baptisms. The first candidate bowed her head over the font as the presider poured water and declared: "I baptize you in the name of the Father, and

of the Son, and of the Holy Spirit." As he spoke these words, all the lights came on. The church became brilliant with light! I must say I have never seen a more powerful illustration of the way baptism releases us from the power of darkness into marvelous light. Weeks later, the parishioners were still congratulating the liturgy coordinator on her effective use of light.

The dramatic power of baptism shown by this incident too often is not experienced. Although I am not suggesting that we contrive an effect like the one above, I do think that an emphasis on the Holy Spirit may make a difference in the way we experience sacraments.

Sacraments are meant to be relational: we encounter Jesus Christ in the Spirit, we are led to the kingdom of the Father, and we grow in unity with the whole church. Any time we emphasize the role of all three persons of the Trinity we are underscoring the relational component of the sacraments. And so this chapter employs an historical approach, for the roots of baptism show the importance of the Holy Spirit's role in this sacrament. (I will primarily refer to baptism in the context of RCIA rather than infant baptism, as the RCIA more clearly illustrates the roots of Christian baptism.)

An outpouring of the Spirit of Yahweh was an important part of Israel's eschatological hope. A general bestowal of the Spirit had long been associated with the Messiah, who was to be preeminently the bearer of God's Spirit. When the Spirit "rested" on Jesus at his baptism, it bestowed on him a continuous endowment of authority and power. Christ's possession of the Spirit, which fulfilled the traditional expectation of the Messiah, had as its immediate consequence the declaration of his status as the Son of God.

A baptism in Spirit

From the baptism of Jesus in the Jordan, to the baptism of Jesus' disciples described in the Christian Scriptures, to the rite of initiation experienced at our own baptisms and at the Easter Vigil, baptism has always been associated with death and with the Holy Spirit. The baptismal accounts of Luke, Paul, and the church fathers show the initiates risking a kind of drowning, namely, a death to self. In the Rite of Christian Initiation of Adults, when the candidates believe that through death comes life they can continue their journey of initiation and receive the Spirit in baptism. Throughout history the experiences of initiation have shown the initiates that death is life and that baptism is the gift of the Spirit.

Already in Jesus' baptism we see that the Spirit is more important than the baptism (water bath) because the Spirit descended when Jesus came out of the water. The Spirit's resting on Jesus and the voice declaring "You are my Son, the Beloved" (Lk 3:22) make sonship and possession of

the Spirit identical, in effect. For Luke, the sonship of Jesus works itself out in the mission of the suffering servant.

When the Spirit drives Jesus into the desert, Jesus wrestles with the implications of being the *Christos*, the anointed one. How is he to use the power of the Spirit? What awaits him as the suffering servant? Is there an alternative mission? No, Jesus states, "I came to bring fire to the earth, and how I wish it were already kindled! I have a baptism with which to be baptized, and what stress I am under until it is completed!" (Lk 12:49–50). For Jesus, the baptism by which he was appointed Messiah and filled with the Spirit equipped him for his saving mission, which would be fulfilled on Calvary.

The early community

Following the lead of Jesus, the early Christians risked dying in order to rise in baptism, thus participating in the Spirit-anointing of the Christos. Paul closely associates baptism and the gift of the Spirit: "He saved us, not because of any works of righteousness that we had done, but according to his mercy, through the water of rebirth and renewal by the Holy Spirit" (Ti 3:5). The intimate connection of Christ with the believer's possession of the Spirit is at the heart of the apostolic tradition of preaching: it is by virtue of the Spirit-anointing of the servant that the Spirit's gifts are granted to the church's members.

The events recounted in the Acts of the Apostles show that the gift of the Spirit makes a person a Christian. Actually, although repentance and baptism are necessary, it is the reception of the Spirit that is the decisive mark of the Christian. Christ's presence in the Christian is proven by the Spirit: "And by this we know that he abides in us, by the Spirit that he has given us" (1 Jn 3:24). Like Jesus' baptism, the baptism of Christians prefigures death, gives sonship, is formed in a covenant, bestows the Spirit, makes the recipient part of a people, and is the proleptic moment which sums up all the consequences of one's union with Christ, gradually unfolded throughout life and revealed in the *parousia* (second coming).

Various theologies

There are various theologies of baptism in the Christian Scriptures. Johannine writings, for example, have a theme of rebirth. The letters of Paul stress dying with Christ and sharing the pattern of his resurrection. In Romans 6, Paul links baptism with death and resurrection. Baptism leads into Christ's death. Paul even invents the new word "with buried" or "con-buried" to show that we have new life only because of the dying. In Colossians 2, we are "con-risen," because baptism is a moment of sharing resurrection. For Paul, the Spirit is virtually identical with the risen Lord.

The theme of dying continues in the church of the first three centuries, when the catechumenate lasted three years. During this time the candidates may have had to change jobs, because persons with certain types of employment (e.g., actors, gladiators, and teachers) could not be baptized. There was no kiss of peace between the faithful and the catechumens. They did have a Rite of Election, which is the origin of our present-day scrutinies. There were pre-baptismal and post-baptismal anointings. Specific details are found in the *Apostolic Tradition* of Hippolytus and the *De Baptismo* and *De Spectaculis* of Tertullian, which give the actual rites that include renouncing the devil, entering the water, and being pushed under the water by the hand of the bishop. (These documents are the basis for our RCIA.)

Dramatic effects

When Christianity was made a legal religion in the fourth century, greater emphasis was placed on the dramatic effects of baptism. What was omitted in substance from the rites of the first three centuries was made up for in dramatic effect. Lent became a baptismal season for everyone, not just the candidates.

Several new features came into baptism at this time. First, the *disciplina arcani* (the handing-on, in secret, of the Creed and other Christian teachings) became more elaborate in what could be seen and known. For example, instead of saying "This is my Body" in the presence of candidates, the instructor would say, "This is my this." Catechumens left the assembly each week after the Liturgy of the Word. The core of initiation was made so sacred and secret that it was not explained until after the rites of initiation were complete.

This secrecy required a time of *mystagogy* (an explanation of the rituals after baptism) and a very expressive initiation rite so that the symbols could speak for themselves. Great emphasis on dramatic effect saw terms like "awesome rites" and "hair-raising" used to refer to the moments of baptism and eucharistic *epiclesis* (calling down the Spirit). In addition, there was more contemplation of the objects used in the initiation rites, for example, oil, water, and fire.

The Easter Vigil of the fourth century was truly a dramatic presentation. It began with an opening (*apertio*) imitating Jesus' *ephphatha* (Mk 7:34). Then the candidates faced west to renounce the devil and blow him away. Next, they made a contract with

Christ, called "adhesion": "I enter into your service, O Christ." There were several anointings which signified the bestowal of both the Spirit and Christ almost synonymously, exorcisms, and the blessing of the font before the baptisms. Candidates were then immersed in waist-deep water, bowing forward three times after questions about their belief in the Triune God.

After the baptisms, the candidates had their feet washed. They were then given a white garment to wear for the next seven days, during what was called "the shining week." Confirmation, the kiss of peace, congratulations, and the reception of a lit candle by the newly baptized concluded this part of the initiation. Now the new Christians were ready to continue the initiation ceremony, and enter the church building for eucharist.

A sense of belonging
With the decrease in the number of adult baptisms, the rites of initiation became less dramatic after the fourth century. When the Second Vatican Council, in the *Constitution on the Sacred Liturgy*, called for the restoration of the rites, the Rite of Christian Initiation of Adults (1971) sought once again to make initiation a powerful experience. The underlying purpose of the RCIA is to generate a "Spirit"-ed people ready to fulfill their mission in the world. Included in this people are not only the neophytes but the entire community of the faithful, who are called to make the journey to baptism with the candidates.

One of the most important effects of initiation is the sense of belonging. Paul attests to this: "For in the one Spirit we were all baptized into one body—Jews or Greeks, slaves or free—and we were all made to drink of one Spirit" (1 Cor 12:13). From the first century and into the new millennium, the Body to which we belong is Christ; that Body is ourselves. Throughout the centuries baptism has been both participation in Christ and participation in the church, the people of God.

As powerful as a sacrament is, the ritual moment is ultimately only a moment. It is in living out the life of Christ on a day-to-day basis in our own lives that the sacraments are fully realized, actualized. As Paul writes in his letter to the Philippians (1:21): "For to me, living is Christ." Do your students see baptism as more than a water bath cleansing us from original sin and giving eternal life? Do they see baptism as an encounter with God that should change them forever, in the way a near-drowning experience would deeply affect them?

Even though the event that gave meaning to baptism was Jesus' own baptism in the Jordan, baptism still is primarily a paschal sacrament in that it remembers the victory of the cross and the resurrection. Baptism is our way to be delivered from the tyranny of death by being crucified with Christ. But it is also a sharing in the resurrection and the pentecostal gift of the Spirit. Baptism is the beginning of initiation, a process that reaches fulfillment in eucharist. It is a conversion process to become the Body of Christ; it is in eucharist that we become what we receive, according to the writings of Augustine.

On that Holy Saturday night some years ago, those of us who knew about the power outage may well have prayed, "Help my unbelief." And God came through: the unplanned coincidence of light breaking into darkness at the moment of baptism achieved the inexpressible.

Prayer

If possible, show a video or slide presentation of water scenes while slowly reading the following prayer.

Baptism,
sign of new life through Jesus Christ,
uniting me with God and the people of God;
allow me to participate in Christ's death and resurrection.

Wash away my sin.
Give me new birth.
Enlighten me.
Clothe me in Christ.
Renew me by the Spirit.
Flood me with salvation.
Immerse me.
Drown me.
Bury me.
Crucify me.
Fully identify me with the death of Christ.

Then set me free.
Raise me up.
Give me new power.
Fill me with newness.
Give me the confidence of resurrection.
Send me out as a disciple
bound to other disciples,
signed and sealed in the same Spirit.
Extend your gifts through us—

gifts of healing and prayer,
gifts of unity and reconciliation,
gifts of faith, hope, and love.

Thank you, O God, for baptism.
Help me grow into its demands
to the full measure of Christ.
Moments of sprinkling,
lifelong commitment.
Common responsibility,
personal response to gifts.
Christians made, not born,
transformed into a new creation,
modeled on the likeness of Christ.

Christians on a journey,
following in the footsteps of the Master,
marking milestones
until all are one in Christ.

Can you hear the echo:
"I am with you always"?

Activities

1. Traditio symboli: handing over the Creed

When the catechumenate was at least three years long, it was not until the Lent preceding a candidate's baptism that he received instruction on the *disciplina arcani* (teaching which the church considered secret, and for which Christians had been persecuted in the past). In one ceremony candidates received the Creed, which had to be memorized (as putting it in writing would risk betrayal of the secret). The bishop or his representative would teach candidates the Creed in phrases, a process called "handing over the Creed" (*traditio symboli*). Later the candidates had to repeat it in a ceremony called "giving back the Creed" (*redditio symboli*) which took place at the beginning of Holy Week.

The *traditio symboli* and *redditio symboli* could be adapted for classroom use.

• Hand over the Creed to the students by discussing its content phrase by phrase. If the Creed has not been memorized, encourage students to do so. They can then "give back the creed" at a later date. (Since most people are familiar with the Nicene Creed, which is the prayer used at Mass, you might want to use the Apostles Creed for this exercise.)

• You can also simulate the experience of the ancient church by having students memorize useful religious information that will be part of the curriculum later in the year. Some examples could be the Ten Commandments, the Beatitudes, or the gifts of the Holy Spirit.

2. Symbols

Every sacrament has its own unique symbols. The special symbols of baptism are the white garment, a candle, water, the oil of catechumens, and chrism.
Have the students employ these symbols in some kind of artistic project. They might be given a piece of white cloth to design a baptismal garment, or a card-

board tube to create a baptismal candle. To stress the element of light as well as the third stage of RCIA, which is sometimes called "illumination," make stained glass windows that incorporate symbols of baptism. (These can be made with tracing paper and magic markers.)

3. Baptismal water

Use baptismal water to bless one another. With drops on one's fingers, have each student make the sign of the cross on another person. A student could also use a branch dipped in water to sprinkle one other classmate or the whole class.

Say a blessing such as, "In the name of Jesus Christ, live your baptism in your daily decisions and actions." Students may ask one another how they could better live their baptism, then pray for that particular grace.

4. Simulating a baptism

Divide the class into groups of four, representing parents and godparents. Extra students may be lectors and greeters. The teacher should be the presider. Let the groups give a name to their imaginary baby.

Start the ritual of baptism outside the classroom to represent persons entering the church building and being greeted. After students are seated as they would be in church, begin the ritual of baptism. Each student should have a copy of the outline or the actual ritual. (You can obtain a baptism ritual from the parish office or diocesan liturgy office.)

5. Giving up the old way of life

Ephesians 4:17–24 speaks about putting on the mind of Christ, renewal, undergoing a spiritual revolution by putting on a new self. Discuss the revolution that should take place through baptism. Ask the students questions such as: what would be your thoughts if you had the mind of Christ? What would you want your new self to be?

These questions could lend themselves to an art project, where the students draw someone with a "new mind," a person who is undergoing a revolution. They can show what the "old person" looked like, and then what the "new person" looks like. Cartoon bubbles could show the thoughts of this new person after putting on the mind of Christ.

Notes

CHAPTER THREE

Rite of Christian Initiation of Adults

Journey Toward Christ

Some years ago our school was privileged to have two teachers who were candidates in the Order of Christian Initiation of Adults. We took this opportunity to teach our students more about initiation. Learning what the Rite of Christian Initiation is and supporting these two teachers provided several wonderful activities and became our lenten theme that year.

We had just installed closed-circuit television in the school, so we interviewed the teachers and all watched the program together. The students were happy to hear the teachers express their sincere appreciation of the support the school gave. But they were even more pleased to hear that the example of the staff and students who lived their Catholic faith was the impetus for these teachers to seek initiation into the Catholic community.

The good that came from this hands-on study of the RCIA impressed me, as it did many others in our school. Ever since, I have not let a year go by without some study and involvement of the students in the process of initiation. Because the RCIA encourages all to renew their baptismal commitment, I feel it is important to incorporate this study into the curriculum. It is not necessary that students know the names of every ritual or the technical distinctions between candidates and catechumens.

But students should be aware of the different rituals they may see on a Sunday morning. They should also have some knowledge of who the candidates and RCIA team members are. Above all, they need to know that being a companion to the candidates (even in small ways) is a great way to renew their own baptismal commitment and enliven the parish to which they belong.

The Second Vatican Council restored the catechumenate of ancient times when it established the Rite of Christian Initiation of Adults (RCIA). In the early church, initiation into the Christian religion was a three-year process, time that was spent in evangelization, in testing a candidate's sincerity, and in possibly finding a different occupation compatible with Christianity.

Today's catechumenate usually lasts one or two years. Its four stages provide formation and information. These four stages are precatechumenate, catechumenate, election, and mystagogy.

An in-depth process

The first period, precatechumenate, is a time of inquiry into the Catholic faith for those who have been baptized into another Christian faith, or a time of evangelization for those who are not Christian. This stage is without rituals, formal instruction, or a time frame.

When the person feels a call to conversion, a call to live according to what Jesus taught as understood by the Catholic community, he participates in the actual entrance into the process of initiation, called the Rite of Acceptance into the Order of Catechumens. (Baptized persons seeking full communion with the Catholic community participate in the Rite of Welcoming Candidates.) The catechumenate lasts one or more academic years during which the person, now called a catechumen, learns in a formal manner what it means to be a Catholic disciple of Christ.

The third stage of the RCIA is called election, illumination, purification, or enlightenment. On the first Sunday of Lent, the catechumens participate in a ritual called the Rite of Election or Enrollment of Names. (Baptized candidates celebrate the Rite of Calling the Candidates to Continuing Conversion.) During this ceremony the godparents testify that the cate-

chumens have been responding to the call to conversion.

The period of election, when the catechumens are called "the elect," is an intense period involving scrutinies, presentation rites, and preparation rites. The three scrutinies are held on the third, fourth, and fifth Sundays of Lent. Like the lenten season itself, the scrutinies are an occasion to examine one's motives, uncover weaknesses, and bring out in oneself all that is good.

In the presentation rites, the elect receive the Creed and the Lord's Prayer. During the preparation rites, the elect recite the Creed and publicly affirm their belief in it. Then on Holy Saturday, at the Easter Vigil, the elect receive the sacraments of baptism, confirmation, and eucharist. During the fourth and last stage of RCIA, known as *mystagogy*, those received into the Catholic Church are now called "neophytes." Until Pentecost they continue to deepen their appreciation of the mystery of salvation.

Throughout the stages of the RCIA, the entire parish becomes traveling companions to the candidates on their journey of faith. The closest companions include the sponsors and members of the RCIA team. Catechists (those who teach the classes) also provide companionship. But the entire parish can join the journey by providing a walking stick of prayerful support, as well as a compass of good example and a lively faith.

Prayer

This prayer experience parallels what the elect experience at the Easter Vigil. It should be done in a church by the baptismal pool or font.

Procession to the baptistry and the Litany of Saints

One student, carrying a large candle, leads the class to the baptismal pool or font. During the procession, the leader (perhaps a teacher or an older student) recites the Litany of the Saints (be sure to include the patron saints of the church or school, the diocese, and the students). The litany is completed at the font or pool.

Renewal of baptismal vows

The leader reads the renewal of baptismal vows. All present respond with "I do." (You can find the baptismal vows in the sacramentary or in the rite of baptism.)

Signing with water

Students dip their hands in a bowl of water or in the holy water font, and sign themselves with the sign of the cross.

Prayer for the elect

The leader mentions the names of those to be baptized at the Easter Vigil. All can join in with a spontaneous prayer for them, or use this format:

Leader   We pray for (name), who is going to be received into our church. Keep him (her) in your care, and fill him (her) with the grace of your holy Spirit.

All   Lord, hear our prayer.

Repeat for each candidate.

If students have been praying for certain candidates throughout Lent, they could make up a prayer for the candidate and take turns saying their short prayer.

Activities

1. Lenten program

During Lent, have the students simulate what it is like to be a candidate for baptism. On Ash Wednesday tell the students that receiving ashes on the forehead is like signing up to be a member of the elect; in other words, they are signing up to be part of a group of persons preparing intensely for Easter. Then during the third, fourth, and fifth weeks of Lent, provide prayer experiences similar to the scrutinies, i.e., questions that examine one's desire for conversion.

Encourage the students to practice some form of fasting on Holy Saturday—for example, refraining from television or sweets—so that they may be in solidarity with the candidates who will also be fasting. During one of your lenten classes, you might want to try a version of the presentation rites, where students receive a copy of the Creed, or are asked to memorize a prayer (the way the elect memorized the Creed and Our Father in ancient times).

2. Solidarity with the candidates

Do some long-range planning with the RCIA coordinator and team to involve your class with the candidates. The students might attend one of the RCIA sessions or participate in some activity with the candidates. The class might be present at one of the rituals, such as the scrutinies. Candidates might share their conversion stories with the class. Students could "adopt" a candidate for whom they pray daily and send occasional "I'm thinking of you" messages. The class can write letters of welcome to the newly initiated at Easter time.

With the liturgical coordinator and the head of RCIA, plan ways your class might be involved in the Easter Vigil. Students could hand out programs and candles at the door, serve at the altar, escort the candidates after their baptism, play a musical instrument, and/or be part of the welcoming assembly. Some of the students might offer free babysitting during the service.

Notes

CHAPTER FOUR

Confirmation

Ongoing Faith

Recently, a parent of a teenage boy wrote a letter to me shortly after a religious event I helped organize. The father mentioned that when his son came home after this event, he could not stop talking about the experience. At one point the son said, "Now I know why people followed Jesus." Might we believe that this boy, who had been confirmed a few years before, had just experienced discipleship—maybe even faith—for the first time?

This event brings home the fact that all of us—young or old—can continually grow in faith and discipleship. Further, overemphasizing the spiritual maturity which is "expected" to occur after receiving the sacrament of confirmation may be a mistake, because all sacraments help us grow into the maturity of Jesus Christ. The grace of the sacraments—any sacrament—may remain rather dormant until one has an experience similar to the event mentioned above.

Confirmation is not a second baptism. Nor is it a reward for attending classes, memorizing questions and answers, or performing a certain number of service hours. It is surely not a graduation ceremony that marks the end of religious education. Neither is it a rite of passage. It is not the first time that the Holy Spirit is part of the candidate's life. Yet confirmation is often regarded in these ways, especially when the sacrament is conferred in either the eighth or twelfth grade.

These false notions may stem from the fact that in today's pastoral practice, baptism is usually separated from confirmation by a period of ten to fifteen years. Instead of being the second step in the initiation process—following baptism and preceding eucharist—confirmation has come to be seen by many as a second baptism, or a graduation ceremony.

How did the sacraments of initiation become separate? A brief history of confirmation will be helpful.

A turning point

There is little distinction between baptism and confirmation in the New Testament. When Peter baptized, he said, "Receive the Holy Spirit." From the very beginning the church has seen the Spirit as the gift of baptism. Further, the bestowal of the Spirit and the bath in baptismal waters have similar effects. Usually the water bath comes first, but in the conversion of Paul, the Spirit was given before Paul was baptized by Ananias.

In the ancient church there were three components within one integrated rite of initiation: the proclamation of the risen Lord, the sending of the Spirit, and the water bath. This integral initiation is found in two aboriginal models from the East and the West. The eastern model (Syrian-Armenian) is composed of an anointing on the forehead, triple immersion in the name of the Trinity, and the reception of eucharist. The western model is similar but adds other steps: instruction, sending out the devil, triple immersion in the name of the Trinity, anointing with chrism (following Tertullian's *De Baptismo*) or the oil of thanksgiving (following Hippolytus's *Apostolic Instruction*), the laying on of hands, and the reception of eucharist.

Difference in tone

Although similar in their components, the eastern and western models are different in tone; for example, the East stresses adoption and birth, while the West stresses death and regeneration, according to the text in Romans 6:3. All ancient documents referring to initiation generally show that initiation is one unified rite in which the coming of the Spirit is more important than the water bath. (That anointing by the Spirit is more important than the water bath is first seen in the baptism of Jesus.)

Despite the integration of initiation, the three sacraments of baptism, eucharist, and confirmation began to be separated by the fourth century. In the *Apostolic Constitutions* (350), a document written by an anonymous Arian, we see a longer initiation ceremony where two or three anoint-

ings taking place at various times. At the time of Cyril of Jerusalem (died 387), there was a long process of initiation before and after the conferral of the sacraments at the Easter Vigil. The initiation process became highly ritualized in the fourth and fifth centuries. "Awesome rites" of "hair-raising" (*phrikodos*) initiation replete with many symbols and rituals took place over the course of several weeks. In the Easter Vigil, for example, candidates turned west to renounce Satan, then east to accept Christ. They were anointed away from the assembly, but also anointed in the midst of the assembly. After the Paschal Vigil, they entered a period of continued reflection called *mystagogia* on the rites they had experienced.

A changing time frame

In the fifth century, when the doctrine of original sin was emphasized, the initiation of infants became common. Parents wanted their children baptized quickly lest the babies die unbaptized. The widespread need for "emergency" or "clinical" baptisms led to initiation in the absence of a bishop. Throughout most of Christendom, except in Rome, the presbyter took over the bishop's role. Although the bishop consecrated the oils, the presbyter performed the rest of the rite, including the post-baptismal anointing. In Rome, however, the second anointing was reserved for the bishop and performed by him at a later time.

The Roman way was eventually imposed upon the whole western church by Charlemagne in 789; that is, priests baptized and the bishops confirmed. Although the delay between baptism and anointing was slight in Rome, the delay between baptism and what came to be called "confirmation" grew longer elsewhere due to the rarity of the bishop's visits. Many parents neglected the brief ceremony of confirmation, which did not seem vital. To rectify this, age limits were imposed. Generally, candidates for confirmation were one, two, or three years old. There was a maximum age of seven for receiving the sacrament of confirmation, but soon the maximum age became the minimum age. By the end of the medieval period seven years of age or older was thought an appropriate time to be confirmed. Children were still admitted to communion at baptism; consequently, the order of the sacraments now was baptism, eucharist, and confirmation.

A question of age

Two interpretations of the sacraments of initiation emerged that altered the timing and placement of the sacraments. People looked upon confirmation as an opportunity to receive an additional grace to strengthen Christians against the battles of life, making them "soldiers of Christ."

Also in the twelfth century the doctrine of realism sprang up. This doctrine, which emphasized the presence of Christ in the eucharistic elements, led to questioning whether children should receive holy communion. It was decided that because children might not be able to consume the host with reverence, they should not admitted to communion until the "age of discretion."

By the Council of Trent in 1552, infant communion was abolished. Confirmation and eucharist were given at a later age with eucharist following confirmation. Initiation was no longer a process but three distinct rites. Generally, baptism occurred shortly after birth, confirmation at age seven, and first communion later. (By the nineteenth

and early twentieth centuries, this was at age fourteen.)

It was Pope Leo XIII (1878-1903) who established the standard age of seven for confirmation. Now the order of sacraments became like that of the ancient church: baptism, confirmation, and eucharist. This changed, however, when Pope Pius X (1903-1914), allowed children to receive first eucharist at the age of seven. Then the order became baptism, eucharist, and confirmation.

This order of the rituals continues today in many places, although some dioceses are requiring confirmation before first eucharist. (These dioceses place confirmation in grade one or at the same celebration as first eucharist.)

Modern practice

The 1971 rite uses the word "postponed" until the age of reason to show that originally confirmation was conferred with baptism. According to this new rite the age of seven seems optimal, with the possible conferral of confirmation on the day of first eucharist, thus preserving the order of baptism, confirmation, and eucharist. Keeping the order seems appropriate, for it allows the Order of Christian Initiation to be "normative." (All three sacraments are given together at the Easter Vigil for those who go through the Order of Christian Initiation.)

Having two separate rites (one for baptism, the other for confirmation) is not wrong. Theologically and pastorally, however, two separate sacraments are not well founded. Yet whatever practice is adopted, the Spirit will act as the Spirit wills, and the candidate will be initiated into Christ, the primary sacrament.

Today we see confirmation against two backdrops: the historical-theological and the pastoral. Since Vatican II the church has wrestled with the theology of this sacrament. Where should we put it? What does it do? Does it even have theological and historical foundations? Regardless of one's answers, confirmation is a ritual moment that expresses ongoing faith. As Christians we live the life of Christ from day to day in constant dying and rising. If Christian spirituality means putting on Christ, then whatever we do becomes a way to live out the life of Christ.

Teachers should inform their students that the stance they take at confirmation should be the one they take with their lives. The mystery of Christ celebrated in confirmation must be the mystery they live. All preparation for confirmation should prepare students to live the life of Christ and reflect upon their relationship with him. Classes, activities, and prayer services will be their best when they help students grow as Christians, putting on Christ and his Holy Spirit.

Prayer

Select several students to be readers, and give them their parts to read ahead of time. Divide the rest of the class into two groups, Side 1 and Side 2.

Leader "You will receive power when the Holy Spirit has come upon you; and you will be my witnesses...to the ends of the earth" (Acts 1:8).

All Holy Spirit, come to me in power and strength. Give me the courage to witness Christ despite pressure to hide my faith.

Reader *A reading from the Acts of the Apostles:*

When the day of Pentecost had come, they were all together in one place. And suddenly from heaven there came a sound like the rush of a violent wind, and it filled the entire house where they were sitting. Divided tongues, as of fire, appeared among them, and a tongue rested on each of them. All of them were filled with the Holy Spirit and began to speak in other languages, as the Spirit gave them ability. Now there were devout Jews from every nation under heaven living in Jerusalem. And at this sound the crowd gathered and was bewildered, because each one heard them speaking in the native language of each. Amazed and astonished, they asked, "Are not all these who are speaking Galileans? And how is it that we hear, each of us, in our own native languages?"...All were amazed and perplexed, saying to one another, "What does this mean?" (Acts 2:1–12).

All O God, continue to give gifts. Fill our hearts with the love of God, bring us together in one faith, and make us holy.

Side 1 Lord Jesus Christ, you told your disciples that they should not fear, for the Holy Spirit would be with them. Give us your Spirit that we may know what to say and do whenever our moral principles or Christian beliefs are challenged. Do not let us give in to pressure and fear.

Side 2   Lord Jesus Christ, your Spirit came in amazing ways. We believe that you can do amazing things in us also. Keep us open to your gifts that we may be instruments of peace, healing, and reconciliation in our families, schools, and neighborhoods.

Side 1   Lord Jesus Christ, through baptism, confirmation, and eucharist we become members of your body. Help us understand how closely we are bound to the church. Give us the desire to support our church and use our gifts in church involvement.

Side 2   Lord Jesus Christ, make us more like you. May we put on your mind and open our hearts to your word. Let us serve with your hands and speak comforting words with your voice. Help us live your Beatitudes and follow the values you taught and the actions you modeled.

Leader   Jesus rejoiced in the Holy Spirit and said, "I thank you, Father, Lord of heaven and earth, because you have hidden these things from the wise and the intelligent and have revealed them to infants" (Lk 10:21). Let us praise and thank God for the gift of the Holy Spirit.

After each phrase, please respond, "We praise and thank you, O God."

         For a spirit of wisdom…
         For a spirit of understanding…
         For a spirit of right judgment…
         For a spirit of courage…
         For a spirit of knowledge…
         For a spirit of reverence…
         For a spirit of wonder and awe…
         For a spirit of healing…
         For a spirit of speaking in tongues…
         For a spirit of love…

Leader   Let us pray…

All   Lord Jesus Christ, you have given varied gifts to the church. Build up your people in love and unity. Let us do what we can to build up the kingdom of God. Help us bring unity to our families, classes, and all the groups to which we belong. Thank you for your gifts to help us achieve these goals. Amen.

Activities

1. Laying on of hands

Several sacraments, including confirmation, employ the laying on of hands to symbolize a transmission of power. Discuss how students can use the power of their hands for good. Draw a pair of hands, and on each finger write one way to use hands for good over the course of ten days.

2. We are the gospel

Remind students that they are the only gospel some people read. Have each student draw a Bible on construction paper and fold it to look like a book. Inside the "book" students may put their photos as a reminder that they—and the lives they lead—are the only gospel some people read. Have them write chapters in the book, one chapter for each gift of the Spirit. The "chapter" would be a prayer to use the gift well or a paragraph explaining how they use the gift in their lives.

3. Affirmation

On a chalkboard or a large sheet of paper, write out the many gifts of the Holy Spirit (these can be found in Is 11:1 and 1 Cor 12:7–12) . Next, have the students write their names across the top of a paper. Circulate these papers around the room, and let the other students write down one gift of the Spirit which they feel the particular student possesses. This could also take the form of an action sentence; for example, "(Name) uses the gift of_____by_____."

4. Lives of the saints

Students might research the biography of the patron saint of their baptismal name. They could then prepare a brief report to share with the class. After students give their reports, a small group of students could use the written reports to make a game such as a crossword puzzle. Or, they could write an acrostic or another kind of poem based on one of the gifts of the Holy Spirit.

Notes

CHAPTER FIVE

Eucharist

We Are Both Diner & Dinner

The liturgy team in our school took a survey of all the students to see how our school liturgies might be improved. It was interesting to note that often the students wanted "special features...holy things, like sprinkling rites." Students had a sense that vibrancy in liturgy comes from longstanding rituals and not "gimmicks."

Although we are always working to get the students to sing louder or respond more enthusiastically, we should work equally hard to educate the students to understand that eucharist is a celebration of the paschal mystery. To do this, it helps to know a little of the development of the eucharistic celebration through the ages. This chapter will give you a deeper appreciation of the eucharistic liturgy by studying the meaning of the words "body" and "blood." We will also look at a little history of the first eucharistic celebrations in the homes of early Christians, and recall the importance of self-surrender (*kenosis*).

Commercials and doctors tell us that we are what we eat. Just as our meals are transformed into our bodies, the eucharist transforms us into the Body of Christ.

Your students may better understand the meaning of the Body and Blood of Christ by knowing what Jesus, as a Jew, meant when he said: "This is my body," and "This is my blood." For Jesus and the Jewish people of his time, body (in Hebrew, *basar*; Aramaic, *bisra*) meant "one's whole self." "This is my body" thus meant "This is my whole self." At the Last Supper Jesus said, in effect, "The bread you now eat is my body, and after my death you will continue to feed on me. When I am gone, you will embody my spirit and message to the world. When you eat in memory of me, you will be reminded that you are my life for the world."

The Aramaic word for blood (*dam*; in Greek, *haima*) means the essence of personal powers. "This is the cup of my blood" means more than the wine equaling the blood of Christ. This is particularly true

This chapter relies on ideas presented in Assembly, *volume 18, number 3, May 1992, particularly "The Cup of Blessing" by Nathan Mitchell; "The Rituals of Diner" by Andrew D. Ciferni, O.Praem.; and "Sharing the Cup" by Edward Foley, Capuchin.*

when we note that there is no New Testament account that simply says, "This is my blood." Rather, all accounts speak of the "blood of the covenant." Because the covenant was made by the death of Christ, the precious blood given at the Last Supper refers to the whole Christ in view of his impending death. When Jesus said, "This is my blood," he meant, "This is me in the act of dying."

Moving from the equation "bread=body" (and nothing more) and "wine=blood" (and nothing more) to "bread=Jesus' whole self" (and much more) and "cup=covenant sealed in blood" (and much more) helps us understand the connection between eucharist and life while underscoring the importance of partaking of the cup.

An intimate relationship

Ask your students about the most meaningful eucharistic sacrifice of their lives. Some will mention their first communion day. Ask them about their memories of that day. Was it a joyous celebration? Do they remember what they were thinking of that day? Were any of them thinking that they were being initiated into a community whose sacrificial meal commits them to life in the same self-giving manner as Christ—who gave everything, even his life? Probably not.

At the time they first receive the eucharist, children are usually too young to realize that receiving the Body and Blood of Christ allies them with Christ's death. The intermediate and teen years are times when we begin to realize the commitment that receiving eucharist requires.

To see the extent of such a commitment, it may be helpful to reflect on what the early Christians were thinking as they partook of their eucharistic meals. We need to go to Paul's first letter to the Corinthians to read the earliest account of the eucharist. This account speaks of abuses that had crept into a gathering for eucharist (see 1 Cor 11:17–34). Paul's anger over these abuses gives us insight into his belief that we can validly receive the consecrated bread and wine only when we are acting like the Body of Christ.

The small Christian communities of the first century met in homes on Sunday evenings to celebrate eucharist. Before the celebration of eucharist, at which the head of the household probably presided, there was a potluck-style meal. In order to accommodate everyone, some sat in the main dining room (called the *triclinium*), while the rest of the group sat in the atrium. Special guests may have been given places of preference, an action which could have led to divisions in a meal that was supposed to be a sign of unity. If poor Christians came, they may have had no food to share. If some came late, there may have been little food left.

Paul was very upset about the gluttony, rancor, and factions, and wrote: "For all who eat and drink without discerning the body, eat and drink judgment against themselves." Paul questioned the very authenticity of the eucharist: how can Christ be present in this Body when the persons gathered for eucharist are not acting like the Body of Christ? The selfishness of those who ate and drank more than their share demonstrated to Paul that instead of identifying themselves with Christ's dying, some Christians were satisfied with merely eating and drinking food marked with his name. And so Paul made clear to the Corinthians that they had to be food for others if their eucharist was to be authentic.

Becoming the Body of Christ

Diner and dinner: this is what eucharist makes us. Jesus Christ is both diner and dinner; we, his followers, must be the same.

Think about the violence that goes into the act of eating. Animals are hunted down, then killed for their meat. Fruit, vegetables, and grain are torn up by the roots or cut down, then sliced, squashed, and so on. At our meals we sit "armed" with knife and fork, ready to spear our meal and shovel it into our mouths.

Look at the violence in our language about food: we spear an olive, cut the meat, stab a potato, chew the food. The fact that a meal is simultaneously an "act of violence" may be the reason why Jesus unfolded the paschal mystery within a meal. For here there coexists imagery of death and violence with life and nourishment; here what is dead—food—rises in a transformed state, that is, our nourished and replenished bodies. We are transformed by Christ's dying and rising through the eating of his Body and Blood given to us through the sacrifice of his life and his exaltation in glory.

But the process of becoming Christ as it is begun in baptism is slow and ongoing. Every time we come to the table of the Lord we take a bit of consecrated bread and a sip of consecrated wine. Yet we are hungry, still. The eucharist does not satisfy us. We want more, more, more. We might even imagine ourselves at the table demanding more: "Give us dinner!" And God may say to us, "Be yourselves the dinner. You must be the bread the world needs. And you can do it, too, because you are transformed. You are the Body of Christ." (You may want to find the passage—called the *epiclesis*—in the Eucharistic Prayer that asks the Holy Spirit to transform the people into the Body of Christ.)

God calls us to become food for the world at every Mass, when we are told: "Do this in memory of me." Do what in memory of Christ? We often think this means gathering to eat in memory of Jesus. Yet the phrase "do this in memory of me" encompasses the whole life of Christ, his attitudes, words, actions. It really means, "In memory of me, you must live your whole life as I lived mine."

The kenosis of Jesus—and us

Christ gave himself up to God in an act of complete self-surrender called *kenosis*. If we live his whole life, we, too, are called to kenosis. We are called to feed others by giving up—surrendering—ourselves. How can we who partake of the Body of Christ not become like Christ, who gave himself as dinner even as he dines with us? How can we be present at a liturgy which transforms bread and wine into the Body and Blood of Christ and not be willing to transform ourselves from someone whose very being feeds others? What may sound like cannibalism is really kenosis.

The ways we surrender ourselves become the test of how well we have entered into the eucharistic sacrifice. While some of these "tests" may include active involvement in the liturgy itself—by singing, responding, and being a liturgical minister—most of the "tests" occur after the celebration, flowing from it. Do we act out of charity towards others? How well do we serve the needs of our neighbors? Do we share the gospel, the good news?

Service and evangelization are the key ways to be dinner in thanksgiving for being diner. They are proof of our covenant with the Lord and with his people.

Prayer

1. Class visit to the Blessed Sacrament

If time and the means are available, take your students to visit Jesus in the reserved Blessed Sacrament. These visits may be as long or short as your schedule allows. While before the Blessed Sacrament, someone could lead a prepared or spontaneous prayer of praise and thanksgiving for the presence of the Lord. Students may also pray silently, but just being with the Lord is a wonderful prayer experience. Time spent this way reminds us that prayer is deeper than words.

2. An illuminated Bread of Life

Give each student one or more verses from the Bread of Life discourse (Jn 6:22–59) that can be illustrated. Have them draw their pictures on construction paper or posterboard, and color with markers, crayons, or colored pencils. After the pictures are completed, read the Gospel passages as students hold up their illustrations.

Use this technique as the basis for a short prayer service by adding a song (or songs), some petitions, and an opening/closing prayer. Or, after each illustration and verse the class can respond: "We praise you, Bread of Life." (Keep the illustrations to use at a later time, or to decorate the classroom space.)

Activities

1. Our personal presence

To demonstrate the importance of investing personal presence at eucharist, have two groups of five to ten students each give a skit or pantomime of an elevator scene. Instruct the first group to act like typical elevator riders, people who look at the numbers, always face the door, and never acknowledge the other persons present.

Instruct the second group to greet each other, talk about sales in the store, maybe even decide to meet for lunch. Ask the audience to describe how the two skits are different. (The difference is in the amount of personal presence invested in the situation. In the same way, we need to involve ourselves at Mass, investing our personal presence.)

2. Outreach to others

The litmus test of good liturgy is the service and evangelization that flow from the eucharist. List all the organizations and committees in the school and/or parish that deal almost exclusively with persons inside the school and/or parish (school council, student council, parish council, and the like). Then list all the organizations and committees that reach out to non-parishioners or persons not directly involved in the school (St. Vincent de Paul Society, support groups, Boy Scouts, etc.).

If the second list is as long as or longer than the first list, the school or parish probably has a good amount of service and evangelization activities in place. A short second list may suggest the need to develop more opportunities to reach out to the community beyond the school or parish. Brainstorm with the students to find ways to better meet the needs of your community.

3. Starting a liturgy team

If your school or parish does not have a liturgy team for students, you may want to start one. This group can be a spiritual catalyst for the school, religious education program, or parish. Besides preparing liturgy, this group could provide opportunities for spiritual growth by decorating the school for Lent/Easter or Advent/Christmas; writing prayers of the faithful for Mass or classroom prayer; by selecting themes and activities with which to observe feasts and liturgical seasons; or by assisting teachers with religious education activities.

You will want to vary the members on your team, making sure you have a good blend of students. Look for differing talents and abilities, as well as personalities. Provide the students with the opportunity to grow in their knowledge of the church and its ministry.

Notes

CHAPTER SIX

Reconciliation

Church as a Reconciling & Reconciled Community

A few years ago our parish celebrated its sesquicentennial. During that year we had a school penance service in which we included reparation for the sins of the past. In the introduction to the service we prayed: "We praise God for the love that has come from our parish over 150 years, and we ask God's mercy for the sins we have committed over the past century and a half, especially our own guilt this year as a school. Since this is the first year of the next sesquicentennial, may our conversion begin the rest of our parish's history in a spirit of renewed love."

Because a sesquicentennial celebration is something bigger than ourselves, its celebrations are, in a sense, bigger than ourselves. This is also true of reconciliation, which must be inserted into the whole work of redemption. This chapter looks at the changes in the celebration of reconciliation as they occurred over the centuries.

A time for penance

The church is a reconciled and reconciling community. Throughout the course of his-

tory, the sacrament of reconciliation has been taken most seriously whenever this aspect of community has been highlighted. In the ancient church it was almost unthinkable that someone would turn his back on a baptismal commitment to Jesus. When grave sin occurred, the community could only hope for God's mercy upon the sinner. As yet, there was no sacrament of reconciliation.

A process of reconciliation after serious sin (called canonical penance) began that paralleled initiation for entrance into the community, with the bishop as overseer of the process. As time went on the process became structured with severe penances lasting a long time, during which the sinner was left out of the community's celebration of eucharist.

If it was determined that serious sin had been committed, the penitent acknowledged his or her guilt and began the period of penance. Those undergoing this process of reconciliation were known as the Order of Penitents. After what was often many years, a penitent would be absolved on

Holy Thursday through communal absolution. He or she would then be able to return to the community in time for the celebration of the Easter Vigil.

In the fifth and sixth centuries, a crisis arose as fewer and fewer people took part in the sacrament of reconciliation. At the same time lay ministers were giving spiritual direction, while Celtic monks would give absolution after private conversations about the spiritual life. From practices such as these private confession began to evolve.

By the time of the Middle Ages the rites of reconciliation were focused on private ritual, rather than on community worship. The process was not geared toward reconciliation with the church, but rather only with God. The laying on of hands, which in the ancient church was a gesture of sharing the Spirit, came to be symbolized by a stole on the shoulder and later, by one hand held up through a screen in the confessional box.

Absolution and conversion

In the tenth century, the steps of the sacrament followed this order: confession of sin, acts of penance, and reconciliation. But the requirement that people return to the church for reconciliation after they had satisfied the acts of penance was not accepted by most people, and the formal ritual of reconciliation fell by the wayside. In time, the order of the sacrament changed to confession, reconciliation, and then acts of penance, and began to resemble modern confession. But two striking changes in the reconciliation process were to occur before we would come to the sacrament we know today; that is, absolution as the cause of forgiveness and absolution as more important than conversion.

The canonical penance of the first few centuries, with its emphasis on rehabilitation and reform, gave way to "tariff penance" which emphasized the security of knowing that one had made satisfaction for one's sins. Tariff penance had a major impact on Western spirituality by making spirituality the means for the salvation of one's own soul. The teachings of moral theology, which were becoming widely accepted at this time, looked more on actions than on motives when putting the soul under scrutiny. Sin and conversion became quantified and largely non-ecclesial.

By the time of the Council of Trent (1545-63), the main focus of reconciliation was on priestly absolution. The elements of reconciliation and conversion were reduced to a ritual which provided grace. The rite of penance was now isolated from community life. This isolation gave rise to important questions: can a sacrament exist as such without a clear connection to the community? Is conversion an individual achievement, or is it known through community living? Can there be purification without transformation? Isn't conversion greater than satisfaction? If sin is central, how does this affect our likeness to Christ, which is part and parcel of spirituality?

Reforms of Vatican II

Studies that led to the reforms of the Second Vatican Council uncovered our ecclesial roots, the community aspect of sin and virtue, and the need to combine liturgy and life. Since the end of the Council in the mid-1960s, we have seen a return to an emphasis on conversion as well as reconciliation with the community. Reconciliation with the church has become more important than the manner in which one confesses sin, and the celebration of communal reconciliation usually includes the acknowledgment of community sinfulness. Today, there is less importance attached to confession and absolution than to making amends with the community.

Yet despite the tremendous amount of research which unearthed numerous theological and historical reasons for communal absolution (a phenomenon that occurred throughout more than a millennium of church history), today individual rites of reconciliation and communal rites often seem to be in competition with each other. Communal rites are sometimes treated as "second best," with individual confession encouraged as "better." The tensions and contradictions between the private rite and the communal rite that exist today, as well as the very limited use of general absolution, will continue to test the teachings and findings of Vatican II in regard to the sacrament of reconciliation.

In the ever-changing evolution of the sacraments, I hope we experience ever more the role of the community in recon-ciliation. When that occurs, we will likely see more use of communal services without individual confession and absolution. We may also see greater use of general absolution not as a way to "get out of confessing sins," but to emphasize how sin and reconciliation are truly communal in nature.

When it comes to penance, efficiency should never be the criterion; it must center on community responsibility. Here, the reforms of Vatican II are a necessary beginning. The 1973 rite of reconciliation is definitely rooted in public worship, a celebration of the paschal mystery. The focus is on God, the emphasis is on Scripture, and the normative structure is communal.

We need to trust this communal dimension as a valid way to celebrate reconciliation. Then we may more readily see that reconciliation is celebrated in every sacrament, for every sacrament brings us closer to God and the community. Every sacrament has the potential to bestow on us all the grace to become a more reconciled and reconciling community.

Prayer

This penance service might be used most appropriately during Advent. Its examination of conscience and use of candles highlight the communal dimension of reconciliation.

Opening Song

Choose a song or hymn familiar to your students.

Opening Prayer

Presider May Christ the Radiant Dawn break upon you!

All His eternal light be also with you.

Student Throughout long ages people lived in darkness and the shadow of death as they waited for the Messiah. He finally came as the Rising Sun to give us salvation by forgiveness of our sins. We come together today to remove darkness from our lives and to receive Christ's light.

Presider Let us pray to receive God's light (pause). Lord our God, our hearts desire the warmth of your love, our minds search for the light of your Word, and our souls long for forgiveness. Give us the ability to grow in love that your light may shine brightly within us. We ask this in the name of Jesus the Lord. Amen.

First reading

Student *A reading from the prophet Isaiah:*

The people who walked in darkness have seen a great light; those who lived in a land of deep darkness—on them light has shined. You have multiplied the nation, you have increased its joy; they rejoice before you as with joy at the harvest, as people exult when dividing plunder.

For the yoke of their burden, and the bar across their shoulders, the rod of their oppressor, you have broken as on the day of Midian. For a child has been born for us, a son given to us; authority rests upon his shoulders; and he is named Wonderful Counselor, Mighty God, Everlasting Father, Prince of Peace.

(Is 9:2–4,6)

All   Sing or recite Psalm 103.

All   Come, Radiant Dawn, splendor of eternal light; shine on those lost in darkness.

Gospel

Student   *A reading from the holy gospel according to John:*

There was a man sent from God, whose name was John. He came as a witness to testify to the light, so that all might believe through him. He himself was not the light, but he came to testify to the light. The true light, which enlightens everyone, was coming into the world. This is the testimony given by John when the Jews sent priests and Levites from Jerusalem to ask him, "Who are you?" He confessed and did not deny it, but confessed, "I am not the Messiah." And they asked him, "What then? Are you Elijah?" He said, "I am not." "Are you the prophet?" He answered, "No." Then they said to him, "Who are you? Let us have an answer for those who sent us. What do you say about yourself?" He said, "I am the voice of one crying out in the wilderness, 'Make straight the way of the Lord,'" as the prophet Isaiah said. Now they had been sent from the Pharisees. They asked him, "Why then are you baptizing if you are neither the Messiah, nor Elijah, nor the prophet?" John answered them, "I baptize with water. Among you stands one whom you do not know, the one who is coming after me; I am not worthy to untie the thong of his sandal." This took place in Bethany across the Jordan where John was baptizing.

(Jn 1:6–9;19–28)

Homily (optional)

Collective examination of conscience

Students representing various grade levels, teams, and organizations, as well as several faculty members, can acknowledge group guilt. After this, students and teachers can continue with an examination of conscience. Here are some examples that can be used in an examination of conscience. Adapt them for your own situation:

We athletes have sinned by_____and we hope to improve by_____.

Our class has sinned by_____and we will try to improve by _____.

We student council members have sinned by _____ and we hope to improve by _____.

We as faculty have sinned by_____and we hope to improve by_____.

Continue with a litany of sorrow such as this:

All   For neglecting our relationship with God through lack of prayer…

Response   We are sorry.

For refusing to take responsibility for our mistakes and instead blaming others…*R.*

For the times we made ourselves the center of attention…*R.*

For the times we used bad language or cheated…*R.*

For the times we caused pain and hurt to others…*R.*

For the times we neglected to do what we could for the poor, the needy, and the lonely…*R.*

For our prejudice and selfishness…*R.*

For misusing our bodies and not showing respect for others…*R.*

For gossiping, criticizing, and lying…*R.*

For damaging property and stealing…*R.*

For disobeying those in authority or ridiculing them…*R.*

For creating divisions in our families, school, or town, or neglecting to do what we can to create unity…*R.*

Now have all participants pray an act of contrition together.

Opportunity for individual confession and absolution (optional)

Optional activity

Before beginning the penance service, have the paschal candle located in a prominent place. Obtain small tapers, enough for each participant; you will also want to have small papers around the bottom of the candles, to catch any dripping wax. (Candles with these papers can be bought through a church goods store or catalog). Place a bucket of sand unobtrusively near the paschal candle in which matches and tapers can be extinguished.

Have each penitent receive a taper from the confessor. The penitent then goes to the paschal candle and asks the person standing there, "Would you help me bring light to the world?" This person lights the candle for the penitent. The penitent then waits there for the next penitent and lights his or her candle. Throughout the time of waiting, students may read meditations provided by their teachers or listen to quiet instrumental music.

Closing prayer

Presider	Lord our God, your light has shone upon us, and we are freed from the darkness of sin. Keep your light in our souls burning brightly while we wait for Christmas, the feast of lights. We ask this through Christ our Lord.
All	Amen.
Presider	May the coming of God bring you the light of God's holiness. May almighty God bless you, the Father, and the Son, and the Holy Spirit.
All	Amen.
Presider	Let us extend a sign of peace to one another, then go out to spread the light of Christ.

You may sing an appropriate closing song to end the service.

Activities

1. Mural of forgiveness stories

Divide the class into groups and give each group a Bible. Have the groups look through the Bible and find stories of forgiveness which they will then illustrate. Give each group a large sheet of paper and some markers or colored pencils on which they can draw their pictures. Hang the finished drawings in the classroom to form a mural, or save them to use as part of a penance service.

2. The roots of sin

Ask the students how many medical problems might have the symptom of headache (or cough, or another symptom). Unless the doctor knows the cause of the headache (or other symptom), the problem is difficult to treat. Maybe the headache will go away, but the underlying problem will remain. In a similar way, much of the wrong that we do is a symptom of deeper problems. It is likely that what may seem to be very different sins—like neglecting prayer, stealing, and using bad language—might have the same problem at their root: pride or laziness, for example.

Let students draw on the blackboard some plants or flowers along with their roots. Write names of sins on the flowers and leaves, but only one common root problem for all of them. Encourage students to look into their hearts to find what may be the root(s) of their sinful actions, and to speak of their root sinfulness when confessing their sins in the sacrament of reconciliation.

3. Guided meditation

Ask the students to close their eyes. Let them imagine that Jesus is talking to them and one other person whom they do not like or cannot forgive. What is Jesus saying to them? How does Jesus treat the person whom the student does not like? How do they find themselves reacting to Jesus' attitude toward the other person?

Tell the students to reach out to Jesus and ask for his help in forgiving the other person. Have them imagine themselves taking the other person's hand and speaking words of forgiveness, such as "I will try to be nice to you," or "Let me learn to accept you as my brother/sister in Christ."

4. Social sin

Talk with the students about their responsibilities as stewards of the world in which we live. You might include thoughts about our responsibility to care for the earth, or about the need to reach out to those less fortunate than ourselves. Discuss ways that they, as young people, can be involved in works of social justice.

Notes

CHAPTER SEVEN

The Church Year

Why Easter Eggs Make Good Stocking Stuffers

One of the most "liturgical" novels that I know is Charles Dickens' best-loved book *A Christmas Carol*. Before the reader says, "Bah! Humbug!" let me explain. When Ebenezer Scrooge is converted, he says, "I will honor Christmas in my heart, and try to keep it all the year. I will live in the Past, the Present, and the Future. The Spirits of all Three shall strive within me. I will not shut out the lessons that they teach."

The mix of past, present, and future is at the heart of the church year (also called the liturgical year). The church year is more than a series of seasons and feasts; it is far different from the secular calendar. The church year is really a metaphor for living the life of Christ: "It is no longer I who live, but it is Christ who lives in me" (Gal 2:20).

Feasts and seasons celebrate the realized future and the already accomplished present, as we remember our past. We do more than repeat feasts year after year as if going in a circle; rather we are spiraling toward the second coming, with each Easter or each Christmas bringing us closer to the fulfillment of the kingdom of God. Like Scrooge, who didn't even know what

month it was after his eventful night with ghosts, we can celebrate every day as Christmas—or every day as Easter, or every day as Ordinary Time—for the only reality we celebrate is the paschal mystery, the mystery of our salvation. Scrooge "knew how to keep Christmas well, if any man alive possessed the knowledge." May that be said of each Christian, too, that we know how to keep every day of the church year well.

This chapter will explain how we live this one reality (the paschal mystery) and will also demonstrate how the church year—or liturgical calendar—developed.

Entering the Mystery

Every day on the church calendar celebrates the same mystery, regardless of whether the day is the Twenty-third Sunday in Ordinary Time, St. Patrick's Day, or even Christmas and Easter. That is the reason why Easter eggs could make good stocking stuffers—at least for a liturgist—because every day is Christmas, every day is Easter, every day is everything. This is true because we have only one thing to celebrate in liturgy; that is, the paschal mystery.

When Jesus ascended into heaven, he did not leave behind lectionaries, sacramentaries, and church calendars. These things took centuries to develop. As a matter of fact, the church calendar is still changing, as the pope adds modern saints to the church year. The church "calendar" (which is not really a calendar, but a means of observing feasts) began with only two feasts: Sunday (every Sunday) and a whopping big Sunday called "Easter." There were only four events which the early Christians celebrated in the first century; namely, Sunday, Easter, baptism, and eucharist. All four of these events celebrated one and the same reality: the paschal mystery.

The paschal mystery is the whole life of Christ: his incarnation (becoming human), life, death, resurrection, exaltation or ascension, and sending of the Spirit. Although there is a historical aspect to the paschal mystery in that Christ died on a cross during the reign of Pontius Pilate, the reality is perennial.

The reality or meaning behind Christ's death is that he offered himself to the Father, and that offering never stops. In other words, Jesus still offers himself to the Father. The reality behind the empty tomb and wrapped cloths is that the Father accepted his Son's offering, and that acceptance never stops: the Father is still accepting the Son's sacrifice.

The Spirit came when Christ died and rose, but the Spirit has never stopped coming. Pentecost celebrates not only the Spirit coming to the apostles, but the Spirit who continually comes to us, as well. The paschal mystery, then, means that indeed, Christ obtained salvation for us through some acts of the past. But salvation still comes to us today as Christ and his Spirit continue to work in us, and the fullness of salvation lies in the future when Christ will come again in all his glory. It is this ongoing reality, which includes a past, a present, and a future, that we celebrate on the church calendar. Whatever the historical reality of church events, we want that same reality to be done in us. For example, when we celebrate the Assumption of Mary into heaven on August 15, we seek the same reality for us—that we will be united with God in heaven. When we celebrate Advent, we desire that the Advent spirit of waiting for the second coming be in us.

Expanding the calendar

As stated before, in the first century there were only two feasts: Sunday and Easter. Over the centuries, other feasts and seasons were added to the liturgical calendar. The first season to be added was a preparation time for Easter. This began as one day, then expanded to two days, a special week, and finally a forty-day preparation period called Lent. At first, this preparation was only for the catechumens. But it quickly changed to a season for all Christians to be in solidarity with those preparing for baptism, as well as a time of discipline for all who wanted to improve their spiritual lives.

About three centuries after the seasons of Easter and Lent became part of the yearly cycle, Christmas was added to the yearly cycle, along with a season of preparation for Christmas which is now called Advent. During the early centuries, the local church communities would remember saints and martyrs on the anniversaries of their deaths. For example, Christians would honor St. Lawrence on August 10, the anniversary of his birth into heaven. Gradually, if the practice became widespread, the feast of St. Lawrence would be added to the calendar.

When the calendar was finally developed, it contained the seasons of Advent, Christmas, Lent, and Easter, along with approximately thirty-three weeks of Ordinary Time. (The word "ordinary" here simply refers to counting, as in ordinal numbers. Ordinary should not be interpreted as meaning "not important.")

The purpose of the church year is to reveal Christ. Every Sunday we come to liturgy begging, as it were: "I want to see you, Lord." Whatever the gospel is for that particular day, it relays to us some aspect of Christ's paschal mystery. For example, at a nuptial Mass, we use readings that have something to say about married love, as well as God's love for us: we are not simply focusing on the married couple.

If we attend Mass on the feast of St. John the Evangelist on December 27th, we are celebrating Christ whom St. John imitated. Similarly, when we come to Mass on Christmas Day, we recall Jesus who was once a baby, but whom we are celebrating now in the fullness of his incarnation—the resurrected, exalted Christ who reigns in heaven. That is why we often hear in liturgy, "Today Christ is born!" or "Today is the day of salvation." Our cause for celebration is that Christ is being born in us—not in Bethlehem.

An ongoing reality
On Easter we say Christ rose today because the reality of the resurrection is what brings us together for liturgy every Sunday: we die and rise with Christ at every Mass. We couldn't have Mass if all we had is history, the events of Christ's life that happened in the first century. But the reality is happen-

ing right here, right now. (This is why historicism really has no place in liturgy; otherwise, we would have the pastor ride down the middle aisle on a donkey on Passion Sunday. But we don't do that, because we only momentarily reflect on an historical happening. Our full attention is on our own following of Christ, now.) Christ's birth is eternally a saving presence in God. We remember a birth in Bethlehem, but we create liturgy from the mystery of the incarnation, the saving reality.

Our church calendar unfolds in a way similar to the way in which Scripture was written—with hindsight to the resurrection. Since the gospels were written several decades after the resurrection, the evangelists could put hints of the resurrection throughout; for example, the Passion according to John has a reference to Christ's seamless garment. Because only high priests wore seamless robes, the reader understands that Christ is the high priest of the New Covenant, even though the words on the surface seem to tell only about a criminal's death.

On the feast of Christ the King we sometimes read about Jesus' death on the cross, but ultimately, this feast of royalty reminds us that the cross is really a throne. Similarly, death and resurrection pervade the readings of Easter: "Do you not know that all of us who have been baptized into Christ Jesus were baptized into his death? Therefore we have been buried with him by baptism into death, so that, just as Christ was raised from the dead by the glory of the Father, so we too might walk in newness of life" (Rom 6:3–4).

The church year is like a kaleidoscope. It always has the same colored stones, but each week there is a different pattern, a different way to see Christ. On one incredible Sunday out of the year we celebrate Christ with Easter eggs and lilies; on another special day we celebrate Christ with Christmas stockings hanging on a mantel at home and poinsettias near the altar in church.

Even though the pattern shifts, every day is an occasion to celebrate the mystery of Christ. Three hundred and sixty-five different ways to see one reality. Truly, we can paraphrase the words of Scrooge: I will honor Christ, the paschal mystery, in my heart all through the year. I will live in the past, present, and future of the incarnate God all the days of my life.

Prayer

The following prayer experiences may be adapted to any feast or season of the church year. Precede the experience by explaining how to use a concordance to the Bible. See if you can have a few Bibles and concordances available for the students to use.

Help the students decide upon a word appropriate for the feast or season. Examples might include the word "heart" for St. Valentine Day, "repentance" for Lent, "light" for February 2 (the feast of the Presentation of our Lord, also known as Candlemas Day), "new life" for the Easter season, "patience" for Advent, and so on. Find several quotations using the exact word (heart) or a derivative of it (hearts, heartfelt). (The teacher might select the best passages beforehand and have the citations on the board or on photocopied papers.) Have each student select a Scripture passage and write it down on a piece of paper or index card. They can then use these with any of the following prayer experiences.

1. Make available to the students slides and one or more slide projectors. Students select slides appropriate to their Scripture quotations. When all the slides are in the tray(s), have a "rehearsal" to make sure all the slides are put in the trays correctly. Then ask the students to quiet themselves for prayer.

All make the sign of the cross. Begin to show the slides, pausing after each one. When the students see the slide(s) they selected, they should read the Scripture quote that goes along with the slide(s).

The effects of juxtaposing a slide with a Scripture quotation can be striking. Use whatever is available for slides, including nature scenes. But try to focus more on pictures of people in the course of daily life, and people from different circumstances and situations. For example, pictures of a picnic, hungry people, or the eucharist might be appropriate for a passage about Jesus feeding the multitude.

If slides and/or a projector are not available, you may want to try this project with pictures cut out from magazines. Give the students each a sheet of paper and a glue stick. Have magazines and scissors at hand for the children to look through for pictures; or, you might cut out pictures yourself and have them piled up for children to look through and choose.

2. Select appropriate quotations for a feast of the church year that is also observed in the secular realm: for example Valentine's Day, St. Patrick's Day, Christmas, the vigil of All Saint's Day (Halloween), Easter, or Shrove Tuesday (Mardi Gras). Ask the students to sit in a darkened room and focus on an arrangement of candles, pumpkins, hearts, figures from a manger, or whatever items are appropriate.

Students can take turns reading their Scripture quotations while background music is quietly played. After the prayer service, make greeting cards for grandparents or residents in nursing homes. Have each person write out their Scripture quotations inside the card. If desired, include a certificate of service or a promise of prayer.

3. Have the students write Scripture passages on index cards, then place them in a box. When students are seated in a circle, pass the box around and let students take one randomly. Softly play instrumental music in the background.

Ask the students to go around the circle, one by one, and read the Scripture passage on their card. Pause several seconds between each quotation. If desired after each passage, the group could say a short prayer such as, "We praise you for your Word" or "Thank you for your words of truth (or joy, love, hope, peace, etc.)." If the word chosen from the concordance is an object-word, such as heart or light, the object could be arranged on a prayer table as a focal point of prayer, or it could be passed from student to student as the passages are read.

Activities

1. Halloween, All Saints, and All Souls

These three days should be seen as a unit, the church's harvest feast of saints. The feast begins with a vigil (Halloween) that has the potential for being a wonderful spiritual experience besides the usual trick-or-treat. Students can make these three days a time of involvement in their parish churches. Here are some suggested activities:

• On October 31 (or on trick-or-treat night), older students may invite the little ones to come in their costumes to church for a brief prayer service. The older students may put on a skit about the saints, particularly those whose lives reflected qualities which the children can imitate; for example, St. Martin de Porres (kindness to the poor), St. Thérèse of Lisieux (prayer), St. Elizabeth Ann Seton (courage), and St. John Bosco (teaching). Another idea would be to compose simple parodies about saints and set them to songs known by small children.

After the skits, someone could lead the children in prayer, and a special blessing be given. The youngsters may then go trick-or-treating or the parish may wish to provide treats and entertainment.

• Older students might help younger students to put together saints' costumes for the liturgy on All Saints Day. After the liturgy the costumed students may wish to visit a nursing home. The older students could accompany them and provide some entertainment.

• On All Souls Day, the students could compose a prayer service for those from the parish who have died. Depending upon the size of the parish, students could read the names of all the deceased or only of those who died during the past year.

2. Feasts of Mary

Every season and every feast celebrates the same reality; that is, the paschal mystery, the saving life of Christ. Whenever we celebrate a feast of Mary or another saint, we look at them as people who lived the life of Christ.

The most perfect model of living the life of Christ is Mary, his mother. Show students that Mary and the other saints were persons who died and rose with Christ, had his attitudes, and imitated his actions.

• Dramatize one or more of the accounts of Mary in the gospels, or dramatize the joyful mysteries of the rosary.

• Live out the spirit of the five joyful mysteries during one week of the school year, preferably in October or May, which are the months dedicated to Mary. Some ways to do this are:

First joyful mystery: The Annunciation
Pray with the students that all of you have the strength and courage to say "yes" to God's requests.

Second joyful mystery: The Visitation
Take the class to visit a nursing home or a group of younger students, just to talk about their lives and yours. How are they different? How are they the same? Or, write out the names of each student in the class. Have everyone pick a name, and swap lunches (or simply eat lunch with that person).

Third joyful mystery: The Nativity
Ask the students to make a list of ways the birth of Jesus has influenced the world. The students might also volunteer to refurbish statues from the parish or school's nativity manger.

Fourth joyful mystery: The Presentation
Have the students bring in their loose change. Use the money to make a donation to a children's hospital or shelter for disadvantaged youth. Recall the wisdom of Anna and Simeon (see Lk 2:22–40), and discuss how you can be open to the wisdom of the elderly.

Fifth joyful mystery: The Finding in the Temple
Brainstorm with the students about some of the ways in which Jesus can be found throughout the day. After this, spend a few minutes in silent prayer.

• Reflect on Mary as the Mother of Sorrows. Have a guest speaker make a presentation on how young people can deal with grief or anger or anxiety or other such emotions.

3. Saint's feasts in Advent

As Christmas approaches, the church celebrates several well-known saints whose remembrance makes the observance of Advent even more special.

• St. Nicholas Day, December 6

Older students could bring candy or another small gift for younger students, placing it on their desks (or in their shoes) before the children enter. As children eat the candy, older students could tell the story of St. Nicholas. Anyone with the name Nicholas or Nicole would receive a special prize.

• Immaculate Conception, December 8

This holy day of obligation remembers Mary as patroness of the United States. Pray for the United States and its leaders on this day.

• Our Lady of Guadalupe, December 12

Hispanic people celebrate this feast of Mary, which commemorates her appearance to Juan Diego in 1531. When he went to his bishop to tell him of his remarkable experience, the bishop was skeptical. So Mary told Juan Diego to pick the roses that grew nearby (this was in December, out of season for roses!), and bring them to the bishop. When Juan Diego opened up his mantle to present the roses to the bishop, it had the picture of Our Lady of Guadalupe miraculously imprinted on it. You might want to teach the students a liturgical song that has both English and Spanish verses.

• Saint Lucy, December 13

Some cultures honor the oldest girl in the family on this day. Surprise the oldest girl in the class with a special treat. Saint Lucy is the patronness of the blind and vision impaired. Find out what you can do to help the vision impaired.

4. The whole picture

The lectionary readings which we hear at Sunday liturgy or during the week give us a specific angle of the whole picture. Thus we might focus on Jesus as miracle-worker one day and storyteller the next. Jesus of Nazareth may be recalled as a babe in Bethlehem in December, but a caller of disciples in January.

Read several gospel passages from several consecutive Sundays. How does each give an aspect of the bigger picture, the paschal mystery?

Notes

CHAPTER EIGHT

Advent & Christmas

Wake Up to the Good Things

Believe me, my lesson plans are not yellowed and brittle from years of use. But I must admit that a few of them are looking "loved to death." These are the plans I bring out every year because I enjoy them so much. When I'm having a good time teaching, the students are usually having a good time learning, too. One such "loved to death" lesson plan is one I do on the first school day in Advent.

I start the class by saying, "Many people give up four things that begin with the letter 's' when they are trying to lose weight or improve their health. Can you guess what they are?" The students keep guessing until they arrive at the right answers: sweets, salt, starches, and second helpings. Then I jump up as if I have forgotten something and say, "That reminds me. I didn't do my aerobics today!" With that I wave the desks back, get the students in the center of the floor, and teach them a few aerobic steps. Then I put on the music, and we have a lot of fun. (The more hip movement I put into it the better the kids like it!)

When the students sit down again (a little out of breath), they are wondering what I am up to. I remind them that many people "watch their weight" to improve themselves physically, but we also need to "watch and wait" in order to improve ourselves spiritually. That is why the season of Advent can be so beneficial to our spiritual health.

A joyous wait

The short, joyous, penitential season of Advent reminds us of spiritual values. It also shows us the wonderful mix of past, present, and future that occurs in all liturgy, throughout the liturgical year. Even as we wait in joyful hope, we are already in the endtimes inchoatively as we proclaim the death of the Lord until he comes. The second coming at the end of the world shows us that the first coming in Bethlehem was not just a visitation, but a permanent presence. Are we awake to the realm of the spiritual, so easily forgotten in our hurried pace? Are we awake to the many opportunities to do the good things that give meaning and purpose to our lives? Advent: 'tis the season to do good things; 'tis the season to be awake to the spiritual; 'tis the alarm clock season of the church year. Indeed, Advent can truly be an adventure!

An *adventus* is an appearance or coming. In ancient times the word referred to pagan ideas of a god or an emperor coming. Now we use the word to indicate three basic manifestations of God: the incarnation, the *parousia* (second coming), and God's constant offer of salvation. Advent deals with faith (our belief in the past history of our salvation), hope (our belief in the future of the second coming), and charity (making God's kingdom come now in our everyday lives through good deeds).

Memory, majesty, and mystery

Advent is the time to become awake to the past, present, and future mystery which we celebrate in December. First, we need to be alert to the past, to the time when the Messiah was foretold. This element of Advent is called memory. The daily readings of Advent are like the church's scrapbook revealing stories of the past. We remember the prophets and kings, Elizabeth, Zachary, John the Baptist, Mary, and Joseph.

(By the way, although the Advent readings are placed first in the lectionary, the season shows us not just the beginning of the liturgical year, but the beginning and the end. It is a circular view, seamless. The First Sunday of Advent, then, is not like a New Year's Day for the church. Strictly speaking, neither Advent nor any other season begins the church year.)

Second, we need to realize that Jesus Christ will come again in majesty. The fact that any day could be the end of the world rarely excites us. Honestly now, did you wake up this morning and say, "Today might be the end of the world"? Members of the early Christian church believed that the second coming would occur in their own lifetimes, and they lived accordingly. Time has proven otherwise, yet this belief used as a basis for organizing our lives and our ministry is still valid today. As we read in Scripture: "Keep awake therefore, for you do not know on what day your Lord is coming" (Mt 24:42).

Finally, in Advent we can become more aware that Christ comes in mystery through every moment of our lives. Just think of the ways that Christ may have come to you in the past few days: in the eucharist, in his word, in the advice of a friend, in the lyrics of a song, in newspaper headlines, in the smile of an older person, in the hug of a child. In every moment of every day God surrounds us with grace.

And while Advent is a time to recall that God comes to us in so many different ways, it is more important that Advent remind us of the ways God uses us to come to other persons. This is why charity is emphasized as the present aspect of Advent. Through our good deeds others will know that Christ is here.

Memory, majesty, mystery: m-m-m, the sound we make at something good to eat. Yes, Advent is a time for good things. Are we awake to all the good that we can do, both for ourselves and for others, during this blessed time? If not, try some spiritual aerobics: they can be very stimulating.

Prayer

These short prayers may be used in a variety of ways, such as beginning classes or meetings, gathering round an Advent wreath, or incorporated into a prayer service.

We praise you, O God, for coming into our midst. Jesus, the fullness of God's revelation, teach us what God is like. Help us become like you. Word of God, be reborn in our lives through our words of faith, hope, and charity. Then help us put these words into action by deeds of service and the pursuit of justice. Help us to continually proclaim the good news of your saving presence among us.

O God, there are so many things we want for Christmas. But the things we really want are rarely in the stores. The malls cannot satisfy our deepest longings. What we really want is to love and be loved. And that is why the best Christmas gift is you yourself, O God of Love.

You have come among us to teach us how to love. God born in a manger, help us to learn that love is humble. Suffering servant, teach us that love is self-sacrificing. Incarnate God, sensitive to human need, teach us kindness and empathy. Resurrected God, fill us with the courage needed to choose wisely. Compassionate God, thank you for the love you bestow on us, grace upon grace, love following upon love.

O God, we wait for so many things—peace in our world, good news, solutions to problems. Lord, grant us patience, the patience of suffering in order to bring about what is awaited; the patience of a vibrant hope that what is awaited will come into being. May we await your second coming in prayerful awareness of the many times you come to us each day.

O God, your Son came as light into the darkness, as a savior of the human race gripped in evil, as a king exiled from his own kingdom, as a warrior in a great cosmic battle to conquer sin and death. Your Son gives us the ability to flower as children of God and as such, become heirs to the continuation of Christ's work.

Illuminating God, help us to be light in darkness when staying in the shadows would be easier. You who conquered sin and death, help us work against evil through constant vigilance. Omnipotent God, help us bring about your kingdom day by day, even when inconvenient or uncomfortable. Never let us be indifferent to injustice. Humble us so that we may share in your divine life.

Activities

1. Making Advent an "Advent"-ure

With the help of your students, make a list of good deeds which they can choose to do during Advent: e.g., offer free babysitting so parents can shop and wrap gifts; clean the house and/or decorate for an elderly person; go caroling in a nursing home or hospital; make Christmas cookies for those who are unable to bake; give money to the needy; and so on.

The adventure in goodness becomes more adventuresome as students use their creativity: for example, youngsters could do hidden acts of kindness, like shoveling snow for the neighbors before they return home from work; or they could make babysitting more fun by making puzzles from old Christmas cards; or they could visit senior citizens to ask them about Christmas past.

2. Personalized Christmas gifts

Encourage your students to use the weeks of Advent to think of ways to make their Christmas gifts more personal. Here are some ideas which you can share with the children:

a. Decide as a family, class, or group of friends to make gifts for each other. When giving the gift, tell the person how you thought of them and prayed for them as you crafted the item.

b. Give a donation to a good cause in someone else's name.

c. Add to Christmas cards an "I care" or "I love you" message, that is, a brief paragraph explaining what the person means to you.

d. Give a gift that keeps on giving; for example, a baked item along with a promise of another baked good every month.

e. Make certificates of service that may be redeemed at any time in the new year.

f. Fill the family stockings with notes of affirmation or poems that let family members know how much they are appreciated.

g. Make a video for family members who won't be home for the holidays.

3. Blessings

Write out a brief blessing prayer, and use it to bless the Christmas tree and crib in the classroom or in the church. Give the students a copy so they can bless the tree and crib in their own homes.

4. Advent alert

On a bulletin board titled "Advent alert" list services that might be provided or gifts that could be purchased for needy families. Encourage the students to pick at least one or two of the items from the list and do what is listed.

5. Parish involvement

Advent is a very busy season for the staff of both a school and a parish. Ask around to see what your students could do to help out in the weeks before Christmas. Some helpful items might include passing out worship aids at liturgies or programs at concerts; stuffing envelopes or sorting out a mailing; bringing decorations out of storage; decorating the church or school; providing refreshments at a parish or school function; and so on.

CHAPTER NINE

Lent

Looking for Life in the Lost & Found

"I like the way we did the first reading today," students often say as they return to class after the Ash Wednesday liturgy. We dramatize this reading from the prophet Joel (2:12–18) by having two students hold scrolls and proclaim the fast, alternating every two or three verses. At various times during the reading a trumpeter standing nearby blows the horn, such as at the line "Blow the trumpet in Zion."

When we gather back in the classroom after the liturgy, I pull out a backpack to illustrate that the journey of Lent can be "a road less taken," to use a line from a Robert Frost poem. I then bring out a box in which I have put some items that will help us on our lenten journey, and add them to the backpack, one-by-one. A Bible and a list of lenten activities make good "maps." A water bottle reminds us that Lent is a baptismal season in which we should pray for those to be baptized at Easter. Our compass is the cross which points in four directions. Our itinerary is a plan of prayer, fasting, and almsgiving. Maybe there is even a change of clothing to remind us to put off our old self and put on the new. (The

clothes are also a reminder to go through our closets as winter turns to spring and give good items to a local secondhand store.)

The lenten journey leads through the desert—a place of struggle where one can meet demons, or an idyllic place where one might come face to face with God. The desert and a journey are two images of Lent which hold much imagery as a guide for our observation of this season. But another lenten image—not on any liturgical list that I am aware of—might be that of a lost and found. This idea echoes what is found in Scripture: "For those who want to save their life will lose it, and those who lose their life for my sake will find it" (Mt 16:25; cf. Mk 8:35, Lk 9:24). Losing ourselves to find ourselves is part of the paradox of Lent.

Losing ourselves in Christ

The New Testament says little about penance in terms of self-punishment; much is said about *metanoia*. Metanoia is repentance that is a radical change of mind and heart where we take on the mind and heart of Christ. We imitate Jesus by putting off our old selves and rising with him. We lose our lives in order to find them. Lent's ultimate penance is changing ourselves into Christ. If we can truly say, "I have been crucified with Christ, and it is no longer I who lives, but it is Christ who lives in me" (Gal 2:20), then we will have found our true selves. (Don't expect this to happen in one Lent, though. A lifetime is required.)

The cross is the ultimate "lost and found." Death is lost in Christ's death; our present life is found, transformed, and made new in the risen Lord. But before we come to the rising we must pick up the cross, and this means transformation into Christ. We die during Lent to become the living Christ at Easter and always. Signed with an ashen cross, our forehead tells the intentions of our heart: I am dead to pettiness and selfishness, and I live life fully with a heart that reaches out like the cross, in four directions. I unite myself with the cosmic Christ, living now, not I, but Christ alive in me.

A change of heart

Imagine the good we can accomplish when we have the mind and heart of Christ! With Christ's mind we have the freedom to make right choices. With Christ's heart we eliminate selfishness and reach out in mercy. Transformed into Christ, we reach out to the cross and embrace it. We look death in the eye and say "yes." We look life in the eye and say "yes." For death and life are two sides of the same coin: "For to me, living is Christ and dying is gain" (Phil 1:21).

Lenten practices—such as giving up sweets, television, or unhealthy habits—are commendable; however, overemphasis on personal penance could make us self-centered. Lent must free us from self-centeredness by putting our mind "on things that are above" (Col 3:2), as well as on justice and charity toward our neighbor. When our minds are on ourselves, penance and self-discipline become spiritual gymnastics ("Look what I did! God better give me a '10'"!). Rather our minds should be on loving God by loving our neighbor.

Performing works of justice and mercy is more important than any asceticism. It is the way we live the first command of the gospel: "Repent, and believe in the good news" (Mk 1:15). We repent; that is, we change our hearts. We lose our hearts of stone and find hearts of flesh, as we live the incarnation of Jesus Christ. Then we can unroll the scroll, blow the trumpet, and announce the good news that now is the day of salvation. What is lost has been found.

Prayer

Invite your students on a journey back into the early days of the church. Ask everyone to be seated comfortably and quietly. Ask them to imagine that they are early Christians who are attending an Easter Vigil. Then read the following account, slowly and prayerfully. Quiet instrumental music may be played in the background.

Imagine that you are living at the time of the early church.... You have never heard of Lent.... There is no forty-day preparation for Easter yet, only an intense period of fasting and prayer called the "bridegroom fast".... In another hour or so you will be celebrating eucharist with the newly baptized....

Although you are eager to meet these candidates and welcome them into the community, you are much more focused on the coming of the Lord. For this is the night on which you firmly believe that Christ will come again in all his glory, as he promised.... Your fasting and waiting are your act of faith in the resurrection and in Christ's coming again.

History books will tell future generations that your fasting is the oldest element of what will be called Lent. But you aren't thinking about making history, for the end of the world is near!... You and your friends believe that Jesus Christ will come again as you wait in vigil; it might be this very night.... So you tell yourself, "Stop thinking about your stomach and how hungry you are. Be ready, for the Lord is coming."

As your stomach longs for food, your ears listen intently to the stories being shared.... The words are very familiar. After all, your great-grandparents knew Jesus personally.... They went to school with Jesus, they saw the lame walk, and they listened to his teaching.... They were spellbound (though a bit skeptical) by the hometown boy who became the Messiah.... Your family's stories are now becoming "good news," the gospel, the *kerygma* that is spreading to more and more persons who want to become Christians.... But to you, these stories are your precious legacy, handed down by grandparents and parents and now shared with your fellow Christians.

Jesus Christ will come very soon.... Be ready.... Pray silently in your hearts.... Tell Jesus how much you desire him to come to you.... Tell him how much you want to be with him.... Tell him your belief in the resurrection and in his second coming.... Spend several minutes now praying silently to Jesus.

Allow about three to five minutes of silent time. Then continue:

There is some commotion at the door.... The newly baptized, with wet hair and faces glistening with fragrant oil, stand shyly, waiting to meet the rest of the Christian community.... It's time for you to welcome the new members of the church.... As you say hello to the new Christians, you realize you are saying hello to Christ.

There will be no second coming tonight.... "Maybe next Easter," you say with a disappointed sigh.... In the meantime, you know that you yourself are to be Christ in the world.

Activities

1. *Passing the cross*

Students stand in a circle and pass around a cross or crucifix. When holding it, students say a word or short phrase that comes to mind as they look at it. Or, you can have each student offer a short prayer of praise and thanks; for example, "Thank you, Jesus, for the gift of salvation."

2. *Hearts of stone, hearts of flesh*

At the beginning of Lent, give each student a stone. Discuss ways to turn hearts of stone into hearts of flesh. Use stories from literature to illustrate the point. Ask the children to keep their stone nearby throughout Lent. During the Easter season, you might want to collect all the stones and put them in a vase with some cut flowers to symbolize new life.

3. *Pantomime*

The gospels for the Sundays of Lent are very rich. Divide the class into groups, and have them silently act out several of the lenten gospels. Ask the rest of the class to guess the story, then read the gospel passage aloud to the class. Discuss how the message of each of the gospels can be applied to our lives.

4. *Paper in my pocket*

Give students a small strip of construction paper to keep in their pockets through-out Lent. At the end of Lent, have the students gather for a prayer service in which they place their construction paper (now probably a bit of fuzz) into a container. Tell the students that the papers have symbolized their dying during Lent, and that these papers will become part of the fuel for the Easter fire. This shows that Easter is brighter for their having been involved in Lent. The Easter fire will continue to transform them into Christ.

Take the container over to the rectory, and ask one of the priests from the parish if they will add the papers to the fire at the Easter Vigil.

5. A lenten survival kit

Have students make themselves a survival kit with items to which they attach appropriate Scripture sayings: for example, a piece of gum to remind them to stick to God (Heb 10:23); a piece of clay (Is 64:8); a chocolate kiss (2 Cor 13:12 and 1 Cor 13:13); and a tissue (Ps 126:5–6). Encourage the students to open their survival kit daily in Lent to read several of the Scripture quotations. During the Easter season, give a reward to those who have memorized their Scripture passages.

Note: Items and citations can be chosen by the teacher and the survival kits simply assembled by the students. The teacher or several parents can provide inexpensive items like band-aids, paper hearts, pieces of candy, paper clips, and straws, using brown paper lunchbags to hold the items.

Notes

CHAPTER TEN

The Sacred Triduum

Three Days, One Celebration

Because the Easter Triduum encapsulates all that it means to be a Christian, our school requires all students to attend at least one of the following during the Easter Triduum: Holy Thursday Mass, Good Friday liturgy, or the Easter Vigil. In this, it is hoped that the students' attendance at the Triduum during the school years will lead to a lifetime of participation, to a belief that liturgy should always be inseparable from the rest of their lives.

The school's parish, knowing that the enthusiasm of youth will contribute to the celebration, asks the students to take part in the Easter Vigil. Students pass out programs and candles, serve on the altar, play musical instruments, help with the wet towels after baptism, and release helium balloons as they lead the procession of newly baptized. They also take part in the other liturgies of the Triduum, as needed. It is indeed delightful to see the students take

ownership for their role in the Triduum liturgies.

In the ancient church the Sacred Triduum meant the time from Friday noon through the time Jesus spent in the tomb. Eventually people spoke of Thursday, Friday, and Saturday as the Triduum. Today we celebrate the Triduum from the beginning of the Holy Thursday liturgy until the end of evening prayer on Easter Sunday. Exact hours are somewhat irrelevant in liturgy, because redemptive time is God's time, and God is outside human time; with God there is no past or future.

Whatever Jesus did within his life here on earth is present in God as an eternal liturgy, expressed as "heavenly liturgy" in the letter to Hebrews. The crucifixion we remember on Good Friday is historical, but the cross is an ever-present reality. The risen Lord still bears the five wounds of the passion. We make a memorial of the events leading to Calvary, but we make liturgy from the self-offering of Christ and our own self-offering assumed into the paschal mystery.

An offering of thanks and praise

When celebrating liturgy we remember the saving events of the past, but we are saved now and we await the future fulfillment of what is already ours. This relationship between past, present, and future is the reason why we cannot separate liturgy from life. Every day we place ourselves before the Lord to praise and give thanks regardless of whether it is the feast of the Baptism of Our Lord or a day in Ordinary Time. Our response to Advent, Christmas, Lent, or Easter—all feasts, all days—should be the same: praise and thanks.

How much of our life is praise and thanks? If very little, we have not allowed the liturgy to come alive in our lives as it should. An attitude of praise and thanks finds physical expression in deeds of faith, hope, and charity. Without these three actions present in our lives there is no meaning in liturgy.

Whether working or playing, participating in Mass or doing service, whatever we do is an extension of the one liturgy—Christ's self-offering to his Father and our participation in it. Thus, everything is liturgical. Once we understand that all is liturgical, once we understand that all we can do is offer ourselves in union with Jesus' self-offering, then there can never be a "business as usual" attitude toward anything we do. We begin to realize that liturgy is more than an hour's ritual in a church building; it is the life of Christ we live day to day.

If we do not commit ourselves to live the life of Christ, we should not even be participating in liturgy, for the purpose of a celebration of eucharist or sacrament is to put on Christ (Gal 2:20). Liturgical celebrations are symbolic moments at which we posit a stance of our whole life. Every moment of our life is eucharistic; everything we do is sacramental. Every second is a vigil for the second coming. As we have said before, the basic focus of every liturgy is one reality; namely, the coming of the kingdom as realized in Christ's death, resurrection, and sending out the Spirit, and as lived by us who die and rise with Christ. Every feast and every liturgy celebrate God and ourselves. More specifically, feasts and liturgies celebrate who we are to become.

A unified whole

The Triduum is one of the best places to learn the sacred unity of life and liturgy. The three days are a unified whole. The three liturgical celebrations of Holy Thursday, Good Friday, and the Easter Vigil on Holy Saturday are really one liturgical celebration. (The sign of the cross and introductory rites begin the Holy Thursday celebration, and there is no dismissal until the end of the Easter Vigil.) During these sacred three days, we should do more than fill up our lives with rituals—as wonderful as it is to participate in all three liturgies of the Triduum. Rather we should fill up our lives with Christ. How can we do this?

One way is by a paschal fast lasting from Holy Thursday until Easter Sunday morning. This may be a fast from food in some form, such as one meal a day or no snacks between meals. The physical fast makes us hungry for the eucharist. But what may be even more effective is a fast from preoccupations that take our focus off the Lord, such as excessive use of media, recreational pursuits, or parties.

Can we remove any clutter from our lives that may prevent the work of God in us? Although Lent may have dealt a blow to our faults and failings, we need to be extra vigilant about our personal habits of sin and virtue during the Triduum. And, of course, taking time for extra prayer is certainly in order.

The best way to live the past, present, and future inherent in every liturgy or liturgical season is to do God's will. Our own lives, as they happen here and now, are the times when redemption is at hand.

May the holiness of the Triduum celebration and the sacredness of every day fill up in us what is lacking until the church patterns its life fully on Christ. That is the purpose of the liturgical year; that is the purpose of the Triduum, the most sacred time of the church year.

Prayer

Have someone slowly read the following reflection. Meanwhile, give each student a small ball of clay, a piece of tinfoil, or some other modeling material. Encourage the class to shape this material into a symbol they associate with the Triduum, such as a cross or a candle.

A single day is not long enough
To celebrate a great event.
Three days are not long enough to celebrate
The paschal mystery, the whole life of Christ.

Holy Thursday,
The first movement of the symphony,
Cries for mercy
And hears Christ's response:
"This is my Body, my Blood."
The psalmist sings in wonder,
"How shall I make a return to the Lord?"
We answer in awe,
"Every time we eat this bread and drink this cup,
We proclaim the death of the Lord!"
The love of a Master clothed in a slave's apron
Requires so much more than the finest ritual.
The new mandate is loving service and serving love.
Christ asks, "Do you understand?"

Good Friday,
The second movement, increases dissonance and tempo.

Like sneers of "Crucify!" and "No, not that one!"
That seem not to affect the Lamb led to slaughter—
So innocent, but so abused that
Even today victims of excruciating suffering find hope.
This servant shall prosper and be greatly exalted.
O Cross, our only hope!
O Cross, sign of our salvation!
Christ asks, "Will you follow me?"

Easter Vigil,
The third movement, crescendo and finale,
Tells stories of creation and killing,
of quick escape and near death experiences,
of death to sin and life in God.
Story's crashing walls lead to baptismal font
Where those who have washed have hope of heaven's kingdom.
Baptized into Christ's death, we, too, live with him.
Christ asks, "Do you understand the empty tomb?"
We look around.
Christ in the newly baptized!
Christ across town, nation, and globe.
Christ closely identified with us.
Rejoice!
Alleluia!

Easter Triduum—
Too much for one day,
Too much for one church season.
Easter Triduum—
The only Christian celebration,
Christ's and our own,
His self-offering and ours.
Christ asks,
"Can you live my life every day?"

Activities

1. Three days, one celebration

Discuss with the students why the Triduum, which seems to have three different liturgical celebrations, is really one celebration. Notice the introductory rites on Holy Thursday and the lack of any formal conclusion at the end of the service. Note the absence of an introduction and conclusion on Good Friday. The services of the Easter Vigil again lack an introductory rite, but they end with a dismissal rite. Thus the three parts celebrated over three different days are really one liturgical celebration.

2. Keeping the paschal fast

Brainstorm about ways that the children can keep the paschal fast with their families. How can they help to create a sacred atmosphere in the home? How can these three days, the shortest liturgical season of the church year, be special and memorable for even the youngest members of the family? Talk about fasting from television and other media, giving time to prayer, attending church services, refraining from quarreling, and helping with household and yard chores.

3. Helping out

Talk with the parish staff to see whether the class could be connected in some way with the celebrations of the Easter Triduum. In the early part of Holy Week students might remove from storage, clean, and polish candlesticks, brazier, or oil vessels. They might put papers on the candles used at the Vigil. Extra greeters may be needed to pass worship aids and candles. Refreshments might be needed after the Vigil.

4. Ending the Triduum celebration

Prepare a special prayer service for the evening of Easter Sunday, which marks the end of the Triduum. This service could be for the parish or home.

5. Sacred time

Offer to help a parish keep the paschal fast of sacred time. If the church building is constantly open for prayer, a morning prayer, for which the students might be lectors, would be appropriate. Students could provide a dramatic Way of the Cross before or after the service of Good Friday. Older students might assign themselves to an hour vigil of eucharistic adoration.

If there is a soup supper during the Triduum, students might help with the serving and dish washing. (Please note: it is inappropriate to have a parish "seder" or agape meal after the Mass of Holy Thursday, because this takes away from the focus on the Last Supper. Also it may be offensive to our Jewish neighbors to re-enact something that is so sacred to them; we would not want persons of other faiths to dramatize a Catholic Mass.)

In trying to get students involved in the services, do not add any actions or elements that are not liturgically correct, especially those things that are merely historical, such as the sound of hammers pounding during the veneration of the cross.

Notes

CHAPTER ELEVEN

Easter

Celebrating the Paschal Mystery

Our school is in session for much or all of Easter week, so I try to make Easter Week special in my daily religion classes. We walk outdoors, find Easter candy in the lockers, start class with a story, and have a week without homework.

While observing the week I ask the students what Easter week and the Easter season celebrate. The response is almost invariably the resurrection of Jesus. Actually Easter is not a feast of resurrection, just as Christmas is not a feast of a birth in Bethlehem, or Good Friday a feast of Christ's death. Easter, like every other day on the church calendar, is a feast of the paschal mystery. A look at the origin of Easter shows that it celebrates more themes than that of resurrection.

Easter is clearly linked to Passover, a feast of liberation. The name of the Jewish feast was *Pesach* (Hebrew) or *Pascha* (Greek), words meaning "leap," because people danced around a pole during this celebration. Later, this leaping was reinterpreted to indicate the "passing over" of the angel of death from the houses of the Jewish people who had marked their doorposts with blood. By the first century the Jewish Passover was a domestic meal linked to the sacrifice of lambs in the temple, a meal which remembered the redemption of the Jews from Egypt and the expectation of a Messiah coming at midnight (Wis 18:14).

The Hebrew Christians adapted the Passover celebration to fit into the paschal mystery of Christ. They observed Easter as a unitary feast that included the passion and resurrection, with an emphasis on the passion. The passion signified both the suffering (*passio*) of Jesus and the passage from life to death (*transitus*). To this celebration they added the resurrection, an event not prefigured in Hebrew Scripture. To see Easter both as a commemoration of the resurrection and in expectation of the second coming proves the feast is both *anamnetic* (remembering the past) and *eschatological* (looking to the future).

A new interpretation

Unlike the synoptics, John's gospel places the death of Jesus on the day when the lambs were sacrificed. The idea that Jesus is the new paschal lamb is reinforced when the legs of Jesus are not broken (Jn 19:33), just as the legs of the sacrificial lambs could not be broken.

By the fourth century, the emphasis on *transitus*, the passage to the Father, takes over. Easter now brings together elements of Passover: a reading from Exodus, a fast until midnight, a late-night meal following the fast, and eschatological expectation. The Jews expected the Messiah to come during the Passover meal, and the Christians expected the second coming to happen at the Passover meal. That is one reason why there was serious controversy over the date of Easter, so that the vigil would occur on the exact day when Jesus was to return.

Also in the fourth century, we begin to see a movement toward a historicized feast. "Do this in memory of me" (the mindset behind the practice of the first three centuries), was changed to indicate: "Do this in memory of the things I have done," referring directly to the historical events of Jesus' passion, death, and resurrection. The paschal mystery became a paschal cycle as St. John Chrysostom wrote: "Two days ago Jesus died. Today he rose." This separation of the paschal mystery over three days would never have occurred a century before.

The redemptive character

This division of the passion, death, and resurrection over several days took away some of the redemptive character of Easter, making it almost solely a feast of resurrection. Mystery became history, and present redemption became the remembrance of Jesus' death. But as a feast, Easter must celebrate mystery, not history. We are not taken back to an empty tomb on Easter.

Rather, we celebrate what is happening among us now, that is, God taking possession of our hearts. Redemption is occurring in us as we enter more fully into Christ. To be a member of Christ is to be a member of the church; only having entered into Christ can a person enter into Christ's prayer and sacrifice at the paschal eucharist.

As teachers, we must integrate memory and hope, passion and glory, *marana tha*—the prayer for the coming of the Lord—and *maran atha*—the confession that the Lord has come—the "already" and the "not yet." We must avoid saying that Good Friday celebrates the death of Jesus, while Easter celebrates the resurrection. Both days celebrate both realities. If this were not so, our faith would be in vain. Please insist that your students refer to Easter as a feast of Christ's dying and rising, a feast which celebrates the whole life of Christ, his paschal mystery—and ours.

Prayer

These reflections and prayers could be used during each week of the Easter season. Because the Easter season somewhat corresponds with the planting season, images of vegetation are used.

Reflection

The mystery of God was fully revealed in Christ, and it is now ours to proclaim. The perennials that die and rise year after year give us a clue about proclamation. They remind us that their cycle is like our own. We die from misunderstandings, quarrels, broken relationships, boredom; we rise in affirmation, friendship, love, and success. We work and rest, hurry and vacation, worry and rejoice. Even our moods rise and fall. Like bi-tonal perennials, we are two shades of the same color, for dying and rising are distinct but one in us. The mystery of God and our own mystery are also distinct but one, for we live in God.

Prayer

Crucified and risen Lord, you died and now live in glory. We share your death and rising, expressing in our own lives your saving work in the world. Help us proclaim the message of salvation with the openness of a flower showing its beauty. May those who see us realize that you live in us, for your brilliance shines forth if we are open to you.

Reflection

"For those who want to save their life will lose it, and those who lose their life for my sake will find it" (Mt 16:25). The doctrine of the cross is a bittersweet legacy of Christ to his followers—bitter in the loss, sweet in the finding. It is the paradox of death being life, crucifixion being salvation.

When we descend to the very bottom of our helplessness, then we can rise to new wholeness and new insight. When we sink to our roots, we have the ground for a new relationship with God and others. Like Jesus who cried, "My God, my God, why have you forsaken me?" (Mk 15:34), we call from the very bottom of our need. In doing so, we have the possibility of rising to new insights, new realities, and new relationships. Miracles happen, life is restored, God's love is released. We have risen.

Prayer

Lord Jesus Christ, suffering servant and risen Lord, help me die to my selfishness and sin. Help me root out the last weeds that choke off my closeness with you. Then let me rise with you to newness of life, and fill me with the sweet fragrance of your Spirit. Wherever I go, may others know the sweet scent of your love.

Reflection

Overturning a rock reveals crawling grubs and squirming worms. Important ecologically, these creatures enrich the soil. They remind us of how much life teems beneath the surface. Overturning the "rocks" of our minds and hearts lets us see life. Removing the stones gives new perspective to old ways of thinking, unchallenged views, unhealed memories, and prejudices. Like the women going to the tomb, we occasionally need to ask, "Who will roll away the stone from the entrance to the tomb?"

To their amazement, these women realized that the stone was not rolled away so that Jesus could get out, but so they could get in. Expecting to see death, once inside the tomb, they saw life in its fullness—the resurrected life of the glorified Christ in which we all now share.

Who will roll away the stone for us? Are we open to new ideas? Do we listen to advice? Are we set in our ways like a rock with a fence around it? Are we open to new ways of seeing? Whose stone will we help remove? Do we share the fruits of our learning, experience, and the insights of our prayer? Do we sensitively risk words that point people in a new direction?

Prayer

Risen Lord, help me remove the stones from my life that prevent me from becoming all that you want me to become. And let me kindly help others remove their stones, so that they can become their best selves. Remove all blocks that hinder life in you.

Reflection

Roots are the unsung heroes of gardens. Does anyone ever "ooh" and "aah" about roots? Yet gardeners know that plant survival is dependent upon this unseen vital source of support and nourishment.

The author of the letter to the Ephesians prays that charity (love) will be the root of his readers' lives. Charity is the great virtue: "And now faith, hope, and love abide, these three; and the greatest of these is love" (1 Cor 13:13). Yet when most itself, charity is quite hidden, unnoticed, unsung.

Think of the times you have experienced love when it meant the most: a child's scribbled drawing, a hug, a compassionate look, flowers or sweets when unexpected, a life-giving conversation with a best friend, or the realization that someone went out on a limb for you. Such times "root" us, give us a place to grow, and help us survive. They are acts of love which, like roots, give support and nourishment.

Prayer

God of Love, by baptism I am rooted in you. Help me live my rootedness in you, and extend my roots of charity to those who need my care.

Reflection

Jesus said, "Consider the lilies of the field, how they grow: they neither toil nor spin, yet I tell you, even Solomon in all his glory was not clothed like one of these" (Lk 12:27). He tells us to stop worrying. Sometimes we beg God over and over again for something, but we never receive it. We wonder, "Didn't Jesus tell us to ask and we will receive?" Then maybe we stop asking and leave the matter to God. Suddenly the request falls into our lap. Removing the worry may give us the receptivity to receive those things for which we ask.

Prayer

God of all trust, teach me trust. Help me learn the lesson that there is no need to worry. Let me be like the flowers which, without undue care, grace the world in their splendor.

Reflection

Some people love to dig in the soil; their hands need to be in the earth. In the spiritual life we sometimes get the urge to dig: "The love of Christ urges us on" (2 Cor 5:14). Moments of dissatisfaction with our spiritual lives occur, causing us to dig a little deeper to hear God's call. "What do you want, Lord?" we may ask.

Maybe the response will be an impetus to acts of service and kindness, or the urge to speak out against injustice. In such moments we discover that we are "a new creation." Made so in baptism, we continually discover depths in ourselves, layers still untapped. God's working in us excavates and hits the nerve of our spirit. Then our spiritual nerve endings pulse with the desire to continue Christ's work.

Prayer

God of all seasons, open us to your urgings and impulses. Bless us with an eagerness to live your life of love. Renew us for the new growth you have planned for us. Help us be your hands and heart. Continue to dig in us until we become a reflection of you.

Reflection

Cyclamen blooming in stony places, honeysuckle climbing porches, maples flashing silver reflect God's glory, but we get just a glimpse, the tiniest peek. God's glory is reflected perfectly in his Son, Jesus: "He is the reflection of God's and the exact imprint of God's very being" (Heb 1:3).

That Jesus reflects his Father perfectly is part of the doctrine of the Trinity. The Father loves the Son with the Spirit, and the Son loves the Father with that same Spirit. As the Father bestows the Spirit on the Son, and the Son bestows the Spirit on the Father, the Spirit proceeds from both.

The Spirit bestowed on Christ is also given to us, allowing us to be by grace what Christ was by nature. Thus we too reflect the glory of God. God shines in our hearts that we might make known his glory.

Prayer

Jesus, splendor of the Father, shine in our hearts that we may reflect your glory. In you we can be good. Give us the grace to reflect you always, the God of all goodness.

$\mathcal{A}$ctivities

l. Searching Scripture

To demonstrate that Good Friday celebrates more than the death of Jesus and that Easter celebrates more than his resurrection, look through the readings of Good Friday and Easter to find themes of both dying and rising on each day. (The Gospel of John is read on Good Friday, because it has the most hints of resurrection in its passion narrative.) In John's Gospel, for example, Jesus is conscious of his pre-existence, and he is not at the mercy of his opponents. Rather we see an omniscient Jesus who has already conquered the world. Look for these examples:

- In the agony in the garden, Jesus does not pray for his Father to save him from the hour; he is ready to drink the cup.

- Pilate is put on trial and is told he has no authority.

- Simon of Cyrene does not help Jesus carry the cross, because Jesus freely lays down his life for his people.

- The seamless garment indicates Jesus is high priest.

- The hyssop indicates Jesus is the new Paschal Lamb.

For other examples see *A Crucified Christ in Holy Week*, by Raymond E. Brown (Collegeville, MN: Liturgical Press, 1986). On Easter Sunday, note the references to dying in the readings from Acts and Colossians, as well as the Easter Sequence.

2. An Emmaus walk

Read the story of the disciples on the road to Emmaus. Then have your students pair off to reflect on questions about the reading, which have been composed beforehand by the teacher. Ask the students to remember that Christ is in their midst.

3. Fifty good deeds

Lent and Easter should be a continuous movement in the church year. Yet so often we fill Lent with good deeds and extra prayer, then omit these practices when Easter arrives. Easter is a wonderful time to continue good deeds, and the spring weather gives us more of an opportunity to be involved in service. Challenge students to do fifty good deeds. Use a calendar with suggestions.

4. Baptismal candle

Prepare a prayer service using the students' baptismal candles. Light them from the Easter candle.

5. Easter candy

Give each student a piece of Easter candy. Have the students share their candy with another student after first stating how that person is like the piece of candy. Example: "You are like this green jellybean, because you are full of life and hope."

CHAPTER TWELVE

Ascension & Pentecost

Waiting for the Clock to Run Out

When one team is very far ahead of its opponents and victory is certain, then playing becomes a matter of waiting for the clock to run out. In a way, Ascension and Pentecost are like waiting for God's clock to run out. We are already living in the endtime; the kingdom is already ours. Victory has already been won. We are simply waiting for the second coming to receive the trophy that is almost within our grasp.

This victory was won in the death and resurrection of Jesus. And so the feasts of the Ascension and Pentecost celebrate the same reality as Good Friday and Easter: that is, the paschal mystery.

Historically, Pentecost has been seen as a season, not a day. Irenaeus wrote in 200 AD that Pentecost is a time when one does not kneel. This clearly indicates that Pentecost is a period of time, not just a day. In 220 AD, Tertullian refers to Pentecost as fifty days of rejoicing, a wonderful time for bap-

tisms. In addition, he sees Pentecost as identical to Ascension, because he equates going to the Father with Pentecost.

Throughout the first three centuries and in the New Testament, Pentecost has many themes: a time of post-Easter appearances, the coming of the Spirit, the second coming, a baptismal period, and a celebration of the same reality as Easter and Ascension. According to the synoptics, the Ascension took place on Easter; according to John, Pentecost also took place on Easter.

A feast for fifty days

Because each Sunday's liturgy is really a celebration of all these events, Pentecost was called the Great Sunday, meaning a Sunday of fifty days. Everything that was signified in a Sunday was signified during this period of Pentecost, because it was the same mystery celebrated; that is, the continued presence of the risen Lord and final victory of Jesus seated at the right hand of

God. According to Origen, we who are risen with Christ are always living in the season of Pentecost. For fifty days we celebrate the result of resurrection. It was only in the fifth century that we began to see Ascension as a separate feast forty days after Easter.

What do Ascension and Pentecost mean today? If we are to be true to our roots, both days should hold the same meaning. And they do: both days celebrate our own uplifting in the Spirit. Baptism has made us alive in Christ, and so we sit with him at the right hand of the Father. Thus, we are already in the kingdom. In Christ we have reached heaven with the head of the Body. We are simply waiting for the clock to run out to experience this fully. And so for fifty days we celebrate this paschal mystery, as our faith and love let the Spirit of God take hold of us.

But as we become more aware that God is taking hold of us, we need to be more open to God's grasp. My favorite definition of a poet is someone who is aware of the present moment. The fifty days of Easter should make us more like poets by helping us explore more deeply God's presence and power in our lives. That is the reason why there is such an emphasis on mystagogy in the RCIA. Not only do the neophytes need a fourth and final stage of their initiation process to deepen their awareness of the mystery of God's presence in their lives; we too need this time after Easter to become more aware of this presence.

Typically our culture deadens our awareness. Instead of watching a movie on a big screen in the theatre we often see it reduced to twenty-seven inches on the television screen. Instead of researching and analyzing the whole national and global scene we

digest only what we read in the headlines or hear in a two-minute radio broadcast. Instead of reading the book we watch the video. Instead of experiencing pain we take pain relievers. Even when we are very happy, we are not supposed to appear too emotional. Yet the fifty days of Easter, Ascension, and Pentecost can help us become alive to the realities of which we are little aware.

Which realities?

The first reality is that the Ascension is not a spatial event like a hot air balloon ride. Jesus was not "down here," then "up there." Rather, the Ascension means that Jesus is fully with us in a much closer way. Now one with the Godhead, Jesus is not imprisoned in the flesh that enforces remoteness. (Jesus lived in 30 AD, not 2000 AD, so we never meet him personally in the flesh.)

Having passed through death to new life, Jesus is as close to us as his Spirit who abides in us. Jesus is as close to us as baptismal grace lets him live in us. Jesus is as close as his Body that identifies itself with us, that is, the church. Jesus is as close as the fullness of God's self-communication. God in Jesus has become, in the words of Karl Rahner, "a sheer openness to the world."

Second, because of Christ's Ascension, the opposite of death is more than life. It takes a lot more than breathing to "get a life." Death is more mysterious than the cessation of brain waves; life is more mysterious than lines on an electroencephalograph. Because of Jesus' death and resurrection, death is no longer something to be feared; its sting is gone. Death is more than mortuaries and cemeteries, bitterness and sadness. Death is the necessary condition through which we come to full intimacy with God. Because of the ascension, the deathbed has become a nuptial bed, the closed eyelids have become full vision, the straight line of a heart monitor has become a straight line to the heart of God. Now that's living! But that kind of living is already ours in liturgy—not quite fullness, but pretty close. And that brings us to the third reality of which we must be aware.

The Ascension does not leave us orphans. After all, Jesus himself said: "I will not leave you orphaned; I am coming to you" (Jn 14:18). How can Jesus be in heaven and still come to us? To understand God's nearness we need to see beyond our horizons. In our rational, everyday lives, it may be easier not to be influenced or engaged by mystery. But sometimes mystery comes into to our lives with power and might, forcing us to take notice, such as in times of birth, death, natural disasters, acts of violence, absolute beauty, literature of the highest caliber, and so on. A certain degree of mystagogy should be latent just below the surface in us at all times, so that we can remain open to wonder.

Having gone through the purgation of Lent, we can use the days of Pentecost to let our sense of mystery lie exposed right up there on our skin. For fifty days we can use the full capacity of our imagination to see beyond the scope of our human limitations...see beyond the constraints of the day to the freedom given God's children...see beyond the idea of sacraments as means to grace, to sacraments as encounters with God...see beyond the Mass as a way to fulfill an obligation, to an opportunity to feast at a heavenly banquet...see beyond a good deed to a way of being Christ in our world...see your neighbor as Emmanuel, God-with-us...see the paschal mystery, eternity, right here, right now...see beyond finding God to experience delight that God is here.

This is the mystery of Easter; this is the mystery of the Ascension; this is the mystery of Pentecost. And this is the mystery of every day, every sacrament, and every season.

Prayer

Giving thanks and praise to God is one of the highest forms of prayer. The eucharistic sacrifice itself is essentially an extended prayer of praise and thanksgiving. God loves our every prayer, so prayers of petition are beautiful in God's eyes. But there is something more selfless about prayers of praise and thanks, for this type of prayer focuses more on God than on ourselves and our wishes.

We can use the letters PRAISE as an acrostic for prayer: primary, raise, acknowledgment, interiorize, seek, and effort.

• *Primary* refers to praise as the highest form of prayer. We pray prayers of praise when we attend the Mass, when we pray some of the psalms, or when we pray any prayers that make God number one in our lives.

• *Raise* is a posture of lifting up one arm or both arms when praying. Raise also refers to turning up the volume on our voices. These physical expressions may feel uncomfortable in the setting of prayer, but we are used to these expressions when watching athletic contests. Raising our arms and voices is like cheering for God.

• *Acknowledgment* involves noticing, affirming, complimenting, and putting the other person first. We acknowledge our mother's cooking with compliments. We acknowledge someone's entering the room by a wave or "Hello!" We acknowledge God by giving God credit for the good things of our world: "Thank you, God, for letting me get that A." "That's a beautiful snowfall. Thanks, God." "Thank you, God, for my ability to dribble the basketball. I appreciate the use of my hands."

• *Interiorizing* means making something part of ourselves, making it so natural that it's like breathing. Can praising and thanking God become natural for us? It

---

The prayer style and ideas used here are adapted from Praising God Daily: The Privilege of Every Christian *by Robert DeGrandis, SSMJ.*

can, if we make it a habit. Try to say, "I praise you, God" or "I thank you, God" dozens of times throughout the day. When you win a contest, say "Thank you, God." When you lose a contest, say, "Thank you, God." When you break a window, say, "I praise you, God." When you do good deeds, say again, "I praise you, God."

• *Seeking* the Lord means that we try to remember God throughout the day, try to see God in every event of the day. When you watch a commercial, talk to God. When you ride your bike, talk to God. When you empty the dishwasher, talk to God. While the computer prints your document, talk to God. Try to find God's presence in all the events of your day. How is God present in the classroom? How is God present near the refrigerator? How is God present in a scolding? How is God present on the soccer field?

• *Effort* is certainly required to praise, raise, acknowledge, interiorize, and seek. Praising and thanking God are not easy prayers, especially when we are hurting. How do you praise God when your grandmother dies? How do you praise God when your boyfriend breaks up with you? How do you praise God when your shoulder becomes dislocated and you miss the championship game?

You do it by just—doing it. "I praise you, God, for the death of my grandmother" might not feel like the right thing to say, but it changes our perspective. We begin to wonder, "What is the good that will come about because of my grandmother's death? How can the sadness and grief make me a better person?" We will begin to see things from God's point of view, not only our point of view. We will take on the mind of Christ, as we are encouraged in Philippians 2:5: "Let the same mind be in you that was in Christ Jesus." And praying with the mind of Christ is the best prayer of all!

Use these steps in a period of prayer. The leader will say the first part of each section aloud, then add spontaneous prayers of your own.

Leader   Let us begin our period of prayer by remembering that God should be first in our lives:
God our Creator, we praise you for creation.
God our Savior, we praise you for salvation.
God our best friend, we praise you for your friendship.

Now offer spontaneous prayer.

Leader As I pray Psalm 150, please raise one or both hands, if you would like to affirm God in this way:

Praise the Lord!

Praise God in his sanctuary; praise him in his mighty firmament!

Praise him for his mighty deeds;

praise him according to his surpassing greatness!

Praise him with trumpet sound; praise him with lute and harp!

Praise him with tambourine and dance;

praise him with clanging cymbals;

praise him with loud clashing cymbals!

Let everything that breathes praise the Lord!

Praise the Lord!

Leader Let us acknowledge the Lord's goodness as we acknowledge the work of God's hands:

For the grandeur of mountains, we praise you, Lord.

For the flow of streams, we praise you, Lord.

For the good feelings of friendship, we praise you, Lord.

For your presence in the eucharist, we praise you, Lord.

Now offer spontaneous prayer.

Leader Let us think of many events that have happened to us throughout our lives, whether as recent as today or years ago. Let us try to interiorize our praise of God for these events, even those events that are still painful to us.

Pause for reflection.

Leader Let us try to seek God in every place and in every situation:

During times of hardship, help us find you, O God.

During times of celebration, help us find you, O God.

When I hear bad news on television, help me find you, God.

When I am honored, help me find you, God.

Now offer spontaneous prayer.

Leader Let us conclude our prayer by promising God our best efforts to live a life of praise and thanks. Try to make a specific resolution.

Pause for reflection.

Leader For the time we just now spent in prayer, we praise and thank you, O God.

Activities

1. Get busy

Ascension means "Don't look up. Get busy!" It is our privilege to continue the work of God. If the physical presence of Jesus were still here, the work of the kingdom would be his responsibility. But the fact that Jesus has gone before us to the Father gives us, the church, the impetus to continue his work and make his words come alive in today's world.

Give the class some ideas and suggestions for service they can perform in the community. Some examples are organizing a clothing drive of spring and summer clothes; offering to do yardwork for the homebound; planting flowers in a section of town that needs color; helping to clean up the downtown area.

2. Extending Easter

Because the Ascension and Pentecost are protracted feasts of Easter, continue the flavor of Easter Sunday over the next fifty days. School liturgies during Easter Week and on Ascension Day should exhibit the "finery" of Easter. Provide a weekly treat for the students, whether no homework during one night of the week or an extra few minutes of social time. Whatever was done during Lent might be enhanced during the Easter season; for example, if students took home a list of lenten penitential practices to follow, have them take home a list of Easter practices.

3. Capturing the moment

If students are good at using video cameras, they might be allowed to film the Easter Vigil and/or other rites during the candidates' preparation. (Video taping should be done inconspicuously without disturbing worshippers.) After Easter they might invite the neophytes and their families (or the whole parish) to watch the video, perhaps while enjoying refreshments. (Slides and photos may be more practical for some classes.)

4. Thank-you cards

As the Easter season draws to a close, students might write thank-you cards to those who have worked hard to beautify the Easter season: sacristans, liturgists, florists, presiders, musicians and singers, the RCIA team, and so on.

5. Counting down

After Jesus went to heaven, Mary and the disciples constantly devoted themselves to prayer in the upper room. Between the days of Ascension and Pentecost, give the students a prayer which can be prayed each day in a special place in their homes. Have them establish a quiet prayer space there and pretend they are the apostles waiting for the Holy Spirit.

Notes

CHAPTER THIRTEEN

Conclusion

Throughout this book we have seen the sacraments as ritual moments in living the life of Christ. We have also seen seasons of the church year as facets of the paschal mystery, which is the life of Christ. As such, the true topic of this book is Christ. But because Christ identifies with his church, the focus of this book is on ourselves, particularly on the ways we are part of the Body of Christ. To conclude, then, we need to emphasize how important it is that we be the hands, voice, and feet of Christ in our world. To do this, we must serve others as Jesus did.

Service is not an option. Service is part of discipleship, the main way in which we live the commitment of our baptism and confirmation. Many of the suggested activities in this book include acts of service, but there are countless other ways to serve. We intercede for others in prayer; we listen to both friends and strangers when they are in trouble; we write cards to the homebound; we vote and express political views; we practice social justice; we forgive; we clean; we attend workshops; we volunteer; the list goes on.

Any time you as a teacher motivate your students to serve, you remind them they are living the life of Christ who came to serve—and not be served.

Remind your students that they are sacraments, for each of them reveals something of God and the nature of the church. Because your class sings at the nursing home, Christ sings at the nursing home. Because a student of yours sponsors a car wash to help earthquake victims, Christ helps the victims. Because you organize service projects, Christ leads the projects. When the church acts, Christ acts. This is the basic truth of liturgical theology; it is also a basic truth of Christian living (Mt 25:45).

Faith in action

When students from our local high school returned after four hours of community service on the Monday before Thanksgiving, they had plenty of stories to share. Those who spent the day in the food bank were amazed at the number of persons who regularly volunteered time there. Students who tutored in the preschool or in the Headstart program were impressed by the brightness and insights of the youngsters. Those who went to the nursing home to put up Christmas trees made comments such as this: "Oh, Sister, you should have met this one lady! She was so friendly and nice, we could have stayed all day with her!"

One girl who visited a homebound person said that she had had a difficult decision to make in her own life; after talking about it with the gentleman she visited, he convinced her of the right decision.

Although the work needed to plan this day had been time-consuming and sometimes frustrating to coordinate, I knew all my effort was worth it when I saw the lasting impact it had on the students. I realized from their stories and experiences that much of what I had attempted to teach in religion class about liturgy had been brought to fruition on this one day of service.

Through the sacraments and the observance of the church year, we learn how to live our lives in reflection of the paschal mystery. We come to model our lives on the life of Christ, God incarnate, head of the mystical body, the church. Through this we understand a little more that all of the life of the church is sacramental. As members of the church, let us live the promise we have been given in the paschal mystery of Christ. This is the challenge of liturgy; this is the challenge of service.

Resources

Bausch, William J. *A New Look at the Sacraments*. Mystic, CT: Twenty-Third Publications.

Cooke, Bernard. *Sacraments & Sacramentality*. Mystic, CT: Twenty-Third Publications.

DeGidio, Sandra. *Sacraments Alive*. Mystic, CT: Twenty-Third Publications.

Kilmartin, Edward. "A Modern Approach to the Word of God and Sacraments of Christ: Perspectives and Principles," *The Sacraments: God's Love and Mercy Actualized*; Giga, Francis A., ed. Villanova, PA: Villanova University Press.

Murphy-O'Connor, Jerome. "Eucharist and Community in First Corinthians," *Living Bread, Saving Cup*; Seasoltz, R. Kevin, ed. Collegeville, MN: The Liturgical Press.

Schillebeeckx, Edward. *Christ the Sacrament of the Encounter with God*. Kansas City, MO: Sheed and Ward.

Schmaus, Michael. *The Church as Sacrament*. Kansas City, MO: Sheed and Ward.

—. *Sourcebook*. Chicago: Liturgy Training Publications.

Taft, Robert. *Beyond East and West*. Washington, DC: The Pastoral Press.